TAKE IT OR LEAVE IT,
It's Only Advice

Erica M. Stephens

COPYRIGHTS

Details in some stories have been changed to protect the identity of those involved. This is an inspirational work based on life experiences.

© 2024 Evergood Publishing All rights reserved.
ISBN: 979-8-9926348-1-5

All rights reserved. No part of this book may be reproduced or transmitted in any form or by any means, electronic or mechanical, including photocopying, recording, or by any information storage and retrieval system, without permission in writing from the publisher.

DEDICATION

This book is dedicated to the One who has been my source of redemption, wisdom, inspiration, and sanctity.

ACKNOWLEDGMENTS

To my three remarkable children, thank you for the profound honor of being your mother. This book is as much yours as it is mine, it reflects the wonder and power of storytelling that you have encouraged me in. Thank you for listening so attentively to my countless stories over the years.

To my husband, you have been the force that pushes me beyond the walls of my comfort zone. In the moments when I might have settled for less, you reminded me that more was always available.

To the friends, mentors, and kind souls who were lifelines in the moments I needed you the most, thank you. Your presence, encouragement, and compassion came exactly when I needed, reminding me that no journey is ever truly walked alone.

THE ISSUES OF A	15
GENERATION	15
THE ERNEST J	28
THE LINE CROSSED	36
THE RIPPLE EFFECT	45
THE CHASE	54
THE BOOKS AND THEIR COVERS	64
THE GRACE DESERVED	73
THE INTENTIONS OF OTHERS	82
THE INSECURITIES	92
THE HELPING HANDS	103
THE FLASHLIGHT CHURCH	116
THE PAIN	124
THE FAMILY BOND	140
THE CHURCH FOLKS	149
THE REPRESENTATYON	157
THE DISMAY	165

THE FIGHT OR FLIGHT	171
THE OBSERVANT	181
THE UNSEEN DESPAIR	192
THE OLD SIN	201
THE SHIFT OF LIFE	210
THE TALK	221
THE UNEXPLAINABLE	230
THE PERSPECTIVE	241
About the Author	244

INTRODUCTION

Imagine a time when the phrase "It takes a village to raise a child" was more than a saying, more than a cliché recited at school assemblies or in parenting books. It was a deeply ingrained way of life. In countless cultures around the world, this idea formed the backbone of society, a living testament to the power of community. These "villages" were not merely clusters of houses defined by geography, they were dynamic, interwoven networks of people bound together by shared values, mutual respect, and an unspoken pact to nurture, guide, and protect the next generation.

But today, those villages are all but extinct, disappearing into the folds of history like fading memories. And so, we are left to wonder what happened. What caused the dissolution of these communities that once played such a vital role in raising children, shaping values, and preserving culture? The answer, like the question itself, is complex, rooted in both the unstoppable tide of progress and the inevitable shift of human priorities.

When I reflect on my own upbringing, I can vividly recall a time when the village still thrived, even within our Western culture. It was not perfect, but it was alive. Back then, mothers and fathers weren't just parents, they were pillars of strength, figures of influence who set the tone for the community at large. Grandparents were not isolated or forgotten, they were living legacies, custodians of wisdom and family traditions. Neighbors were not just the people who lived next door, they were honorary family members, trusted elders whose word carried weight and whose advice was often sought. Children developed in a communal embrace, where everyone shared the responsibility of raising them. A child who misbehaved on the street would not just face a neighbor's stern warning. The news would travel home faster than the child's own feet, carried not by malice but by love in a collective desire to see every child grow into their fullest potential.

And yet, somewhere along the way, this way of life began to crumble. I've often wondered why these villages, which were so integral to the human experience, began to fade. The answer seems to lie in the relentless march of progress. As society evolved, industrially, technologically, and economically, the need for close-knit, interdependent communities diminished. What was once essential for survival and success gradually became irrelevant in a world that prized individualism, speed, and self-sufficiency. The physical closeness of neighborhoods gave way to suburban sprawl. The steady pace of communal life was drowned out by the frenetic pace of modern living. What was once a lifeline became, to many, a relic of the past.

Of course, change is inevitable. As the traditional villages dissolved, we adapted, as humans always do. We created our own modern "villages," smaller and more intimate, often composed of close friends, immediate family, and trusted confidents. These micro-communities are different in scale but not in significance. They still play an essential role, offering support, wisdom, and a sense of belonging.

I, too, have a village of my own. It's not the sprawling network of elders, mentors, and neighbors that it might have been in another era, but it's no less meaningful. My circle is made up of people I trust implicitly, individuals whose perspectives I value deeply. Each member of my village contributes something unique. Together, we navigate life's challenges, drawing on our collective strength to overcome obstacles and celebrate victories.

But even the strongest village has its limits. I learned this firsthand when I found myself facing a trial that felt both overwhelming and deeply isolating. It was one of those moments when you feel as though the weight of the world is pressing down on your shoulders. I turned to my village, expecting answers, guidance, or at least the comfort of shared understanding. Instead, I found myself at a loss. No one seemed to have the wisdom I sought. Their advice, though well-intentioned, felt theoretical, an offering of opinions rather than the hard-won insights I craved.

I was struck by how unprepared I felt to navigate this crisis. For the first time, I doubted not just myself, but the systems of support I'd always relied upon. Was it possible that no one in my life had ever walked this path before? The realization was disheartening. What I needed was the guidance of someone who had truly been there, someone who had faced similar struggles and emerged on the other side.

It was in that moment that I understood something profound. The wisdom we seek in life isn't always readily available in the people closest to us. And yet, it's out there.

The decisions we make, especially in life's pivotal moments, are far too important to leave to chance. Why should we each be forced to learn everything the hard way, as though we're the first to walk these roads? While no two journeys are identical, the challenges we face often share common threads. And while no one can hand you a perfect map, the guidance of someone who has traveled similar terrain is invaluable.

Think about it: if you were planning a trip to a distant, unfamiliar destination, wouldn't you appreciate tips from someone who had been there before? Their insights wouldn't rob you of your adventure, they would enhance it, equipping you with tools to navigate your journey with greater ease and confidence. Life, in many ways, is no different. That is why I feel compelled to share my own experiences through this book. It is not because my perspective is the only one that matters, but because I know how valuable it can be to hear from someone who has walked a similar path. My hope is that my stories and lessons will resonate with you in some way, offering guidance, comfort, or even just a moment of reflection. Take from them what you will, with all the respect and kindness intended. After all, this is just advice, a humble offering from my village to yours. Take it or leave it, what you choose to do with it is entirely up to you.

THE ISSUES OF A GENERATION

Grandma's house was the place in my childhood where I could rely on the few constants in my life. Unconditional acceptance, unrestricted conversation, and a wholesome meal were all guaranteed. Grandma was one of the few people with endless patience for my inquisitive mind and talkative spirit. Grandma's house was also the central location where my extended family would meet up. Uncles, aunts, cousins, and all would gather at grandma's house.

I quickly learned it was also the place the adults gathered to discuss adult business. As the only girl in the family, of male cousins and brothers, I was the only child allowed to be in the room with my mother and the other adults. As long as I kept to the rules, I had an unspoken permit to remain. This largely meant staying out of the adults' conversations and absolutely no commentary on whatever the adults discussed. Sometimes I would get caught laughing at something the adults were joking about. I would get a glance in my direction warning me to redirect my focus to the television instead of the conversation. I did not mind because if I pretended to watch television in the room with the adults, I was usually in the right place at the right time to hear everything.

One night my seat on the living room sofa placed me in the front row to one of the most dramatic scenes of my lifetime. It began with a frantic knock at the front door. Grandma motioned towards the door, but my mother cut her off, insisting on answering it since it was late evening. Anticipating the possibility of trouble, my aunt Sharon stood behind my mother. When the door opened, everyone was relieved to see it was only my uncle James on the other side of the door. Our relief was short lived. James began to frantically ask for my grandmother. Another uncle, Red, nicknamed for the natural color of his hair, appeared. Red had been across the street when he noticed his brother running towards my grandmother's house and decided to check if everything was okay.

James staggered into the full light of the living room, immediately shifting the atmosphere into a panicking frenzy. Under the new light, we could all see James' shirt was heavily stained with blood. The image was as shocking as something out of a horror movie. What soon followed was a steady stream of panicked questions from everyone in the room. James was the youngest of my grandmother's nine children and had a family reputation for being the most dramatic. That night he did not disappoint. As if someone yelled action, his next words were "Mama! Mama! Mama! They got him" followed by his continuous sobs and trails of "they got him." As his body sank closer and closer to the floor. Red did his best to calm his brother down by yelling at him to stop crying and tell us what happened. Through his heightened breathing and broken sobs, James began to tell his story.

Earlier that evening James went downtown to a local bar to have a beer. While enjoying his beer, my uncle Lou happened to visit the same bar. It was a mere coincidence. Lou and James had not planned to meet, but when they saw each other, they decided to catch up over a drink. The evening seemed innocent enough, but it quickly took an unexpected turn. While seated a group of white men started harassing them. Lou and James, feeling targeted, refused to back down. Words were exchanged and soon they found themselves surrounded by the group. My uncles felt there was no choice other than to defend themselves. It was clear this group's intentions were to start trouble. Lou and James were in agreement that although they did not start it, both were okay with finishing it.

A fight broke out and my uncles fought for their lives. James then looked at my grandma and said "momma I did everything I could to walk away but we had to fight. We were surrounded and there was no way around them. I tried to keep Lou beside me, but I lost him in the fight. There were too many of them. I couldn't keep track of where everyone was. I couldn't grab Lou before they got to him. I'm so sorry momma I don't know where he is. The police came and I had to get out of there."

My aunt Sharon was enraged and ready to serve her own version of justice. She was upset that her brothers were targeted while simply minding their own business. My mom could not believe what was happening either, but she was distracted with trying to calm down my aunt. Sharon was in full escalation mode which increased every second her younger brother was missing. After her initial gasp, grandma was silent. She sat there thinking through everything that was said. Red raised his voice over his siblings and told everyone to calm down. "Rushing out blindly won't help anybody. We need a plan," he declared, trying to bring reason to the chaos. He volunteered to take James back to the bar and look around for Lou. The two men left, and the women waited impatiently in the living room. My grandmother took a seat perched at the window looking towards the street as she waited for her sons to return. She rocked back and forth in a self-soothing motion anticipating whatever news she was preparing herself to hear.

    It took a while for Red to return, but he did. We had not been prepared to see him walk in alone. I silently thought to myself that there should have been two if not three brothers returning. Red's composure was completely different. Red walked into the living room and avoided looking my grandmother in the eye. With that move, I knew the news would be bad. Red sat down slowly on the loveseat across the room, facing the sofa I was seated on. The tension and silence in the room was heavy and unbearable. Red inhaled deeply which signaled to us that we should brace ourselves for what we were about to hear. As Red began to speak, I could feel myself leaning in towards his direction. I did not want to miss a word of what was coming out of his mouth.

Red and James went to the bar but did not find Lou. They talked to the bartender who remembered James earlier in the evening. There was a long pause while Lou gathered his strength and composure to continue. Just as James said there was a bad and bloody fight, and the police were called. Sharon who seemed to be on the literal edge of her seat, asked if the group of white guys were arrested. Seemingly frustrated, James exhaled and said "white guys, what white guys? There was no one else there. Those two fools were down there fighting each other." I tried to let that sink in. The group of white guys could not be found because they were not there. They were never there. My uncles had spent the entire day drinking together and were so intoxicated they imagined the whole thing, and they fought one another.

The bartender said the ordeal began with the two of them shadowboxing the air around them and swinging at people who were not there. Eventually one of their punches landed on the other and they began to fight one another. The bartender did what he could to break it up, but they began fighting again. Someone at the bar called the police for help. When the police arrived, Lou was arrested and taken into custody. While back at the scene of the crime, James was spotted and arrested as well.

I was so caught up in the night's events that I had forgotten the rules that allowed me to be seated in the front row to the main event that evening. Without thinking I asked Red "what about all the blood if no one else was fighting?" Luckily everyone was too deep in thought trying to reconcile everything that no one noticed I had broken the number one rule. Red looked pitifully at me and said, "baby girl it was Lou's blood." Lou received the worse end of the fight. James broke Lou's nose in the fight and the blood gushed everywhere. James told my grandmother that he would try to bail both brothers out of jail on Monday. Since this all occurred on a Friday night, they had to remain in jail until Monday when their bail would be set. The mood was somber after that. None of the adults were in the mood to stay and we all went home soon afterwards.

As a child, this was my introduction to generational issues. I was too young to assign a label to what I heard and saw that night. I knew there was a larger issue than a drunken brawl between brothers at hand. My uncles were both very beautifully black, dark-skinned men. The absurdity of them fighting fictional white men who they mistook for one another, was not lost on me. That night provided the largest reference for the alcoholism that I observed in my family on various occasions. As I grew older, memories of that evening did not fade. I could not allow it.

In the years that followed, I recalled that night each time I was offered a drink or a controlled substance. It was clear to me that alcoholism ran in my family. Long before alcoholism was widely recognized as a diagnosable disease, I was aware of the risk. It was one that I could not quite articulate but felt with every fiber of my being. As I grew older and encountered the pervasive presence of peer pressure, it became evident to me that alcohol was a gamble I simply could not afford to take.

If science tells us that alcoholism is a disease, shouldn't we consider genetic predisposition? When heart disease runs in a family, doctors warn against diets and behaviors that could trigger it. Why do we not apply this approach to other generational issues? Religion and what some reference as spirituality also teaches that certain issues and curses can pass through multiple generations. Just as doctors recommend avoiding activities that could exacerbate a condition, spiritual guidance should also give caution.

Being present that night was slightly traumatic, but it allowed me to see how substance abuse and addiction has plagued my family. In hindsight, I was fortunate to have been there, as that night was never discussed again. The adults usually kept anything embarrassing, dishonorable or provocative tucked away, nicely swept under a rug of secrecy and seclusion. It was the way things were handled by most families back then. My cousins and brothers in the next room had no idea of what transpired that evening. I knew telling them was not an option or a risk I could take at the time.

Now as an adult I advocate understanding family history. It is a critical step in making informed decisions about your future, yet many of us are deprived of this opportunity. Too often, families remain silent about issues like addiction, mental illness, abuse, and trauma. Their voices are muted by the weight of societal judgment, embarrassment, and deeply ingrained shame. The silence creates a barrier, leaving individuals to navigate their lives without the benefit of insight into the struggles that shaped their family tree. The truth is that these behaviors, patterns, and challenges are connected by generations, woven into the next generations to deal with.

From a Christian perspective, these patterns are understood as more than mere coincidence or biology. They may signify spiritual strongholds or generational curses that have yet to be addressed. Scripture speaks to this reality, illustrating how the sins and struggles of one generation can ripple through those that follow, creating cycles of pain, dysfunction, and bondage. Yet, it also offers hope: through Christ, these chains can be broken, and families can experience healing and restoration.

Recognizing the patterns in your family history is the first step toward freedom. For me, acknowledging that alcoholism and substance abuse had a foothold in my family was both sobering and empowering. It gave me the clarity to make choices rooted in self-preservation and, later, in faith. Knowing the battles my relatives faced helped me understand that these struggles were not merely personal failures but part of a larger narrative, a narrative I was determined to rewrite.

From a spiritual standpoint, this acknowledgment goes beyond mere observation. It becomes a call to action. Identifying generational patterns allows you to approach them with intentionality, seeking God's guidance through prayer, repentance, and spiritual warfare. These practices are not just acts of faith but also acts of love, for yourself and for those who came before and after you. When you bring these patterns before God, you are inviting Him to intervene, to heal what has been broken, and to break the chains that have bound your family for generations.

In addition to fostering personal healing, understanding your family history cultivates a profound sense of empathy. It allows you to see your relatives not just as flawed individuals but as people who faced battles they may not have been equipped to fight. This perspective can soften your heart, paving the way for forgiveness and deeper connection. Instead of perpetuating cycles of blame and resentment, you can become an agent of unity, drawing your family closer together by acknowledging the struggles you all share.

This empathy extends to future generations as well. By addressing these patterns head-on, you can create a legacy of freedom and faith that your children and grandchildren can inherit. Instead of passing down chains of addiction, fear, or shame, you can pass down testimonies of victory, resilience, and God's transformative power. Through intentionality and faith, your family story can shift from one of generational bondage to one of generational blessings.

For many years, I carried the weight of my family's history without fully understanding it. Now, I see it as a gift, an opportunity to learn, to grow, and to trust in God's ability to redeem even the most broken circumstances. Recognizing the patterns in my family's past did not just save me from following the same path. It led me to a deeper relationship with Christ, who has the power to heal what we cannot. Breaking free from these patterns is not easy, it requires courage, honesty, and faith. But the rewards are immeasurable.

Self Reflection

What struggles or challenges seem to repeat across multiple generations (poverty, overspending, addiction, broken relationships, illness, etc.)?

Do you notice recurring themes in how family members handle conflict, money, parenting, or emotions?

How do family members talk about faith, resilience, or healing?

If you continue on the same path, what are you likely to gain and pass on to future generations?

Growth & Reflection

Discuss ways you can make small changes that will have a large impact.

Journal about your family history to spot repeated cycles.

Have honest conversations with relatives to uncover hidden stories.

Educate yourself financially, emotionally, and spiritually to break cycles.

Use prayer, fasting, or declaring affirmations of freedom from negative cycles.

Participate in supportive communities, faith groups, or healing circles.

THE ERNEST J

Ernest J was a man who always stood out from the crowd. His tall, commanding stature, dark skin, and striking green eyes ensured he was noticed wherever he went. Yet it was more than his appearance that set him apart. There was something intangible, something within him that demanded attention. There was an air of quiet authority, a calm steady presence that hinted at a man who had a lot he could say if it were not for patience and wisdom's interference.

At least fifty years my senior, Ernest J, had clearly lived a life full of rich, experiences. Though he never spoke of his past in detail, I could imagine him as a younger man, vibrant, fiery, brimming with energy and charisma. There is no doubt he had been a force of nature in his prime. Surely someone impossible to ignore, the kind of man whose presence filled a room before he even said a word. And yet, it was not his past adventures that lingered with me.

Ernest had a gift for sharing his knowledge with humility. His guidance never felt like a command or decree. Instead, it felt like a map carefully handed over with just enough detail to set you on your path, while leaving space for you to decide your own direction. In a transactional world where kindness is so often laced with ulterior motives, Ernest's generosity of spirit stood out. There were no strings attached, no hidden expectations. He was simply a man who wanted to see the next generation thrive, a role he adopted effortlessly and without ceremony. For me, his presence was grounding, his insights a treasure I didn't fully appreciate at the time. His wisdom gave me an advantage, like a secret compass handed down by someone who had walked the same treacherous roads of life and knew how to navigate them.

But that wisdom, as I would come to understand, had not come without cost for him. Ernest's body was a living ledger of the sacrifices he had made, the battles he had fought, and the burdens he had carried. His frame, though still sturdy, moved with a deliberate slowness that spoke of long years spent in hard labor. His skin, lined with scars, whispered stories of pain, sacrifice, and survival, stories he rarely told but wore like badges of honor. A fractured spine, a fused vertebra, and the constant companion of his cane were souvenirs of his military years. Each step he took, slow and measured, seemed to remind you of the toll life had exacted from him. Yet he never complained, never sought sympathy. Ernest J carried it all with quiet dignity, asking for nothing more than the respect that was due to him.

When Ernest J spoke, I paid attention. His words, though simple, carried weight. They were distilled truths, honed by decades of experience. I knew even then that his wisdom was a gift I could not afford to take for granted. I first met him at the retail store where I worked. When I was promoted to manager, Ernest was one of the first to congratulate me. Leaning in close, his green eyes fixed on mine, he said, "One of the first things you need to remember is to be firm but fair.

People need to respect you as a leader and being firm, yet fair is the way to earn it." He went on to advise me "don't ask anyone to do anything thing that you as a manager haven't done or wouldn't do yourself". His voice was low and steady, his tone deliberate, as though he were imprinting the words into my very being. He concluded with a slight nod and a faint glimmer of amusement in his eyes, "If you stick to that, you'll be alright."

At the time, his words seemed simple, straightforward advice from an elder. But as the months and years passed, I began to understand their depth. His guidance became a touchstone, a principle that shaped not only my leadership but my character. Ernest had taught me that decisions must be made in good faith and character. It went beyond decisiveness. It was about integrity, about being the kind of person others could trust to make sound decisions, while trusting the direction of leadership.

One day, however, I learned one of Ernest's harder lessons. I arrived at work to find him waiting for me, his expression unusually serious. As I approached, I realized something was wrong. Ernest wasted no time. He had overheard staff repeating details from a conversation that could only have come from me. Without naming names or raising his voice, he delivered a simple truth, "Never complain to someone who isn't in a position to fix your complaint." The blunt truth in his words knocked some sense in me. I realized that my venting turned into, ranting, then complaining. By the end of the conversation, I had accomplished nothing. My problem was unchanged and now had become a topic of gossip thanks to me. He explained that venting to the wrong person gave them power, ammunition for gossip or worse. It was a lesson in restraint and discernment that I practice to this day.

On another occasion, as we stood near the store's large front windows, gazing out at the parking lot, a customized SUV pulled in. Ernest watched quietly for a moment before turning to me and saying, "Traditionally, the wife is supposed to drive the better car." At first, I dismissed the remark as a random comment, Ernest pressed on. He explained that the "better car" was not about status but about reliability. A broken-down car left a woman vulnerable, dependent on the kindness, or cruelty, of strangers. Most often that stranger would be another man or a group of men. "No man," he said firmly, "should let his pride or selfishness put his woman in that position." His point hit me then, it was not about cars, it was about care, responsibility, and selflessness.

Over time, Ernest J's lessons wove into my life in ways I could not have predicted. His wisdom followed me years later into Corporate America, where I often faced frustrations and challenges that made me want to vent. But before I opened my mouth to speak, I would recall his voice, urging restraint. I realized that complaining might soothe me momentarily, but it would not solve my problems and possibly make them worse. Ernest had taught me to focus on solutions I could accomplish, not grievances.

Looking back, I am struck by how much we take for granted the wisdom of those who came before us. In an age that prizes innovation and speed, we often dismiss the elders who carry within them a treasured trove of hard-earned knowledge. Spending time with Ernest J taught me that the core truths of life values like fairness, respect, integrity, and care, are timeless. They are lessons that transcend generations, teaching, and leaving a lasting impact that outlives us all.

I never got to say goodbye to Ernest J. One day, his familiar presence disappeared, his diesel pickup truck no longer parked outside of our store. I am not sure what happened to him, but his words continue to live on. They are a legacy of quiet wisdom that continues to guide me and those who I share them with. In honoring his lessons, I honor him, a man whose influence shaped not just my decisions but my understanding of what it means to live with purpose and integrity.

Times may change, but life remains constant, and there will always be lessons to learn from those who walked the path before us. Through Ernest J I am reminded of the power of listening to such wisdom and holding onto the simple truths that endure. His teachings were not flashy or complex, but they carried a soundness that remains unshakable. With a nod to Ernest J, I continue my journey, fortified by his guidance and inspired to pass forward the timeless lessons he entrusted to me.

Self Reflection

Who in your life has spoken wisdom or guidance that deeply impacted you?

What specific advice, insight, or story did they share?

Are there lessons you ignored or resisted that you should revisit now?

How do you honor or show gratitude to the people who spoke your my life?

Reflection & Growth

What principles or values do you want to carry forward from their wisdom?

How can you integrate this wisdom into your daily decisions, habits, or goals?

Do you plan to one day speak wisdom into others' lives? What motivates you to do so or not to?

THE LINE CROSSED

The seed was planted long ago. It is almost amusing to think about how innocently it began. Who could have guessed that a simple childhood game, played in laughter and carefree joy, could plant the roots of something so complex, so heavy? I certainly did not. As children, we played a game called Telephone. You may have played it too. We would sit in a circle, passing a whispered message from one person to the next. The excitement built as the message traveled from ear to ear, its original form slowly morphing with each retelling. By the time it reached the last person, it was often hilariously distorted, drawing peals of laughter as we marveled at how wildly it had changed.

At the time, the game felt harmless. It was all wholesome fun, or so I thought. But in hindsight, I see it differently. That seemingly innocent game was, in fact, my first introduction to a habit that would later prove destructive. Unbeknownst to me, it was teaching me the mechanics of gossip, the way words travel, the way stories shift and twist, and the way trust can quietly unravel when whispers begin to spread.

As I grew older, the messages I carried were not so innocent anymore. And neither were the consequences. Gossip became more than just a game. Gossip became a habit, a web of whispers that was easy to get tangled in. I will admit, I was drawn to it. There is an undeniable allure to being in the know, to holding a secret or a juicy detail. It is intoxicating, isn't it? The thrill of sharing it with someone else, the power of being the one who knows, it is hard to resist. I found myself swept up in that allure, passing along stories, adding my own embellishments, not stopping to think about the harm I was causing. Even when I felt a twinge of guilt, I brushed it aside, telling myself it was not really a big deal. But deep down, I knew better.

The turning point came on a day I will never forget. A close friend, someone I cared about deeply, confided in me during one of the hardest moments of her life. She poured out her heart, sharing her fears, her struggles, and her insecurities. I listened carefully, offering her comfort, advice, and reassurance. By the end of our conversation, she seemed lighter, more hopeful, as if the simple act of sharing her burdens had helped her see a way forward.

I should have felt proud of the role I played in supporting her. I should have taken a moment to reflect on the trust she had placed in me, to honor the sacredness of her vulnerability. But instead, I gave in to temptation. Without even pausing to think, I picked up the phone and called another friend. The words tumbled out before I could stop them: "Girl, you won't believe what just happened."

The moment the words left my lips, I felt a pang of regret. I knew I had crossed a line, betraying the very trust my friend had placed in me. I tried to justify it to myself. I just needed a second opinion. I told myself someone else's perspective might help. But deep down, I knew the truth. It was not my story to tell. It was never mine to share. I had violated her trust, and no amount of justification could change that.

Life, as it so often does, has a way of teaching me a lesson. Not long after, the tables turned on me. I confided in someone I trusted, a close friend, someone I thought I could rely on. I shared something deeply personal, believing it would stay between us. But it did not. When I found out that she had shared my story with someone else, I felt a wave of hurt and betrayal. How could she do this to me I thought. How could she treat something so personal with such carelessness?

My initial reaction was anger, hot and raw. But just as quickly, another feeling crept in; shame. I realized, at that moment, that I was no better. How could I demand loyalty from others when I had not offered it myself? How could I condemn someone for doing to me what I had done to others? I was forced to confront a bitter truth. I was reaping the harvest of the seeds I had sown.

Life has a way of circling back the energy we put into it, often when we least expect it. It does not forget, nor does it overlook. Instead, it waits patiently, watching as we write our own fate with our choices. I once believed myself immune to the very wounds I inflicted upon others, convinced that certain misfortunes belonged to someone else's story, not mine. But life has a relentless way of correcting arrogance. It hands us the very lessons we thought we would never need.

The betrayals I once dismissed as necessary, or even justified, found their way back to me, not as punishment but as understanding. The pain I caused became my own, and in that suffering, I saw myself clearly. It is a humbling realization. We are never above the consequences of our own actions. What we plant, we will harvest. Sometimes, the most painful harvests are the ones that finally teach us who we really are. Eventually, I grew tired of the drama. I needed separation from the constant tension and hurt that gossip stirred up in my life. I started to reflect deeply on my choices, on the harm I had caused, and on the kind of person I wanted to be. Slowly but surely, I made the decision to change. I stopped engaging in gossip, stopped sharing stories that were not mine to tell. It was not easy. Old habits die hard, after all, but the rewards were immediate. My life grew quieter, more peaceful. The constant buzz of drama began to fade, replaced by a calm I had not realized I was missing.

Through this process, I began to uncover something profound: many of the struggles we face as adults are rooted in seeds planted during our formative years. These issues begin quietly, taking root when we are at our most innocent, naïve, unguarded, and unaware. A seemingly harmless teasing of a child, one who has not yet developed a foundation of security, can grow into an insecurity that festers, only to manifest later in life. The drug addict we might judge or dismiss as an adult may be the product of a seed sown long ago. A seed that blossomed into a desperate need for escape from shame, trauma, or pain. The addiction we see is merely the result, the final branch of what was planted deep within, unseen, years before.

For me, it was a childhood game. Something that seemed so insignificant, so harmless turned out to be anything but. In time, I came to understand the importance of self-reflection: the ability to pause, look inward, and trace the origins of behaviors back to their earliest form. Often, this quiet exploration unlocks a deeper understanding, offering clarity where confusion once reigned, and logic where there was once only chaos. By identifying the seed, we begin to see the roots of who we are, allowing us to grow beyond them with intention and awareness.

This realization that the seeds of our struggles often lie in our past can be both liberating and sobering. It requires courage to revisit those moments, to sift through memories that may feel small, buried, or forgotten. Yet, in doing so, we gain the power to confront the origins of our pain and unearth the truth behind our patterns of behavior.

When we connect the dots between who we were and who we have become, we no longer feel trapped by habits or reactions we do not understand. Instead, we begin to reclaim control over our lives. By tending to the neglected roots of our experiences, we can cultivate new growth; healthier, stronger, and more intentional than before.

Ultimately, this journey of self-reflection is not about blame or regret but about healing and transformation. It reminds us that we are not defined by the seeds planted in our youth, nor are we bound by the harvest they produce. With awareness and effort, we can choose to uproot what no longer serves us and plant new seeds. Seeds of confidence, compassion, and purpose await us all. By choosing so, we give ourselves the freedom to not only overcome our past but to shape a future that reflects the best of who we are and who we strive to be.

Self Reflection

What emotions usually lead you to discuss someone else's private matters jealousy, curiosity, judgment, boredom, insecurity)?

If the person knew what you said, how would they feel toward you?

Does repeating someone else's personal information align with the kind of character you want to have?

Are you speaking about others instead of addressing your own feelings or issues with them directly?

How do you usually feel after sharing details about someone that weren't yours to share?

Growth & Reflection

Do you consider people who repeat other people's personal matters trustworthy or untrustworthy?

What can you do differently when you're tempted to comment on someone else's life?

How could your relationships improve if you only spoke words that showed respect for people's privacy and dignity?

Who in your life models healthy respect for others' business, and what can you learn from them?

THE RIPPLE EFFECT

I was eight years old when I first learned about adultery. Until that day, it was something I had never even thought about. I still remember it clearly as it was the moment adult problems first entered my childhood. Earlier that day, I had gone on a short bike ride with my friend and classmate Louie. He and his family had recently immigrated to the US. At eight years old I could have cared less about where they immigrated from. All that mattered was that we got along, and he was one of the few children in the neighborhood my mother allowed me to play with. We spent an hour playing and riding our bicycles up and down the block. There was no pattern to our play. We were just two little kids enjoying the fresh air and freedom outdoors. When my mother called me home, we exchanged goodbyes and went our separate ways. Unbeknownst to me the day was nearing a sharp turn.

During that time, my mother was in her "no child left behind" era. Wherever she went, her kids followed. This often meant my brothers and I spending our time waiting in the car as my mother ran her errands. On this occasion she promised it would be a quick trip to the department store and back. I quickly put away my bike and joined my brothers in the car. To me, the errands themselves were meaningless chores my mother did. There was usually nothing to these errands beyond boredom for me. Fortunately, this trip was a little different. What made this one special was the promise that we would pick up take out for dinner. Restaurant food was a rare treat usually reserved for special occasions. I had no idea of what was so special about this occasion. I just knew to keep quiet and to behave long enough to receive my meal. My brothers and I waited outside in the car patiently as my mother went inside the store.

True to her word it was a quick errand. We left the store and made our final stop at the restaurant before heading home. When we arrived home, my mother parked in front of our apartment building, and we all headed inside. My brothers went upstairs and my mom to the kitchen, but I remembered something essential. I left my Barbie doll in the car. Without a word, I turned and went back outside to the car. Thankfully, the car doors were not locked. I retrieved my doll from the back seat where I had left her.

As I was heading back towards my front door, I saw a familiar face coming towards me. It was Jerome, our next-door neighbor, and another man running toward the building. As they ran, they were shouting but I could not understand what they were saying. Before I knew it, one of the men picked me up as he was running. I could tell by the fear in their voices they were not the threat. Something else was and it was behind us. As we reached my front door, I caught a glimpse of a third man running toward my direction. Jerome shouted for me to get inside, and then he ran into his apartment next door.

I stumbled back into my home, confused and breathless, calling for my mother. When she found me, her expression shifted from anger to panic. I figured I was in trouble for going outside without permission. I was ready for the chastisement for my actions. What I was not ready for was being pushed to the ground. But there I was, on the floor wondering what I had done to deserve that. When my mother yelled for me to stay on the floor, I was still clueless. It was not until she began yelling at my brothers who were upstairs that I understood what was happening.

Someone outside was firing a gun. The faint pops I heard and dismissed when I was outside alone suddenly took on a sinister meaning. The weight of it all began to settle slowly, as the sirens filled the air, signaling the arrival of police and emergency responders.

My mother waited until the neighbors and curious onlookers gathered outside before stepping out herself. Intrigued, I trailed behind her, unnoticed. Our next-door neighbor, Jerome, who was also the husband of my mother's friend's, spotted me and quickly gave away my position. He turned to me and sternly said, "Next time you hear gunshots, you need to run." I nodded, still processing the muffled sounds from earlier. It was the first time I heard gunshots, a sound I would not forget. Jerome then recounted the shocking events to my mother and the neighbors as the police moved through the apartment complex.

A man from the building behind ours had returned home early from work, only to find his wife in bed with another man. The other man fled, and the enraged husband grabbed his gun. Jerome and his friend were outside when they saw the chase unfold. The other man, desperate for help, ran toward them, but Jerome pushed him away, not wanting to get caught up in his consequences. The woman's affair was a well-known secret amongst the neighbors. Jerome had warned the other man earlier that week that he was playing a dangerous game by sneaking around with a married woman. Jerome and his friend ran away from the scene, towards the front of the apartment complex. The other man ran behind them, and his mistress' husband gave chase. It was then that Jerome spotted me, directly in the line of fire.

Without hesitation, he picked me up and rushed me to safety as the husband fired shots at the fleeing man behind him. Jerome then speculated that the wife must have called the police, afraid of what her husband was going to do. Someone must have pointed out Jerome to the police because they interrupted his recounting of events for him to give his witness statement.

It was not until later that night that the reality of what occurred earlier began to sink in. My brothers reminded me over and over that I could have been killed retrieving a doll. I knew that was incorrect. My life had been endangered because of the actions of other people. That night, the air buzzed with hushed conversations and heated debates. Some neighbors felt the husband had overreacted, endangering innocent lives. Others believed his actions were justified, given the circumstances. There were even whispers of disappointment that the wife and her lover had appeared unscathed. As an eight-year-old, it all seemed like a chaotic mess to me. The husband was arrested and taken to jail, while the wife secluded herself in her apartment, avoiding the neighbors' judgmental stares. Her lover gave his statement to the police and left, as the neighborhood continued to buzz with retellings of the events.

Over the years, that day has replayed in my mind more times than I care to admit. Before that moment, I believed, as many do, that what happens behind closed doors is no one else's concern. It is a convenient lie, one we tell ourselves to stay uninvolved, to feel secure in the illusion that someone else's choices will not touch our lives. But that day shattered that belief. I learned that private choices do not always remain private. Their consequences can ripple outward, seeping into lives far beyond the walls where they were made.

Each time I hear the word adultery, the memory surfaces, sharper than I expect. I think of emotional love and the extraordinary, fragile power it holds set against the betrayal that can so easily destroy it. How love and betrayal can be on two sides of the same thread, a thread stretched so thin that the slightest break can snap it entirely. Adultery goes beyond a mere betrayal of trust. It is a reckless gamble with the human heart, a force far more dangerous than we care to admit. The heart, capable of breathtaking loyalty, kindness, and passion, is also capable of unspeakable rage when broken. Betrayal can awaken something primal, something uncontrollable inside even the gentlest of people.

We often think of adultery as a personal failure limited to one or both parties in the relationship. That is a lie. Infidelity is not contained within two people. The ripple effects are the most cruel to the innocent. A momentary thrill, a single decision, can unleash consequences more devastating than anyone ever imagines. Much like a fired bullet, there is no control of the ricochets.

If you ever find yourself tempted, if the thrill of secrecy ever beckons you, whispering its empty promise, stop. Pause. Ask yourself: is a fleeting moment of pleasure worth the deep, unrelenting pain it will leave behind? Is it worth breaking the heart of the person who trusts you? Is it worth risking everything including your family, your stability, your peace, for something that will disappear as quickly as it came? The relationships you take for granted may crumble into disrepair under the weight of your choices.

If you ever find yourself standing on the edge of temptation, remember nothing you gain will ever outweigh what you stand to lose. Secrecy fades. Passion cools. But the pain you inflict will last. Choose integrity, even when it is difficult. Choose honesty, even when temptation calls. Choose love because it is sacred. Protect the bonds that matter most, and guard them fiercely before a moment of impulse becomes a lifetime of regret.

Self Reflection

What actions have you taken that have had a ripple effect of consequences for others?

What motivated you to take the action you did? Was it intentional, emotional, or reactive?

What short-term effect did your choice have on you (emotionally, mentally, physically)?

Did your action align with your values, or did it go against them?

Growth & Reflection

What lessons can you learn from the outcomes of your actions, positive or negative?

What choices have you made in the past that you are proud of because they brought good results?

How do you want your future actions to reflect the kind of person you want to become?

THE CHASE

May 29 was supposed to be a good day. Everything had been planned meticulously, down to the smallest detail, and everyone knew their roles. My best friend's mother was throwing her a surprise party to celebrate her sixteenth birthday. The excitement leading up to it had been building for a while. A few weeks earlier, her mother had enlisted me to help with the invitations, a task I took on with enthusiasm. Sixteen felt monumental, like the beginning of a new chapter. I had turned sixteen earlier that month, and my friend and I had spent countless hours imagining what this age would bring. It was not just about the milestone itself but about the dreams tied to it. More freedom, independence, and a sense of stepping into a more exciting, grown-up world was within our reach. To us, sixteen felt like a golden key unlocking a door to the future. The party was a success beyond anything we could have hoped for.

My friend had no idea what awaited her as we led her into her backyard, where a crowd of classmates, friends, and family yelled, "Surprise!" Her shock quickly turned to joy as the DJ played her favorite songs, and we danced under the glow of string lights that crisscrossed the backyard. The music was loud, the energy contagious, and the party was non-stop. It was not just a birthday party, the timing made it much more. With the school year ending in a few days, it doubled as a celebration of the end of the school year. It was the last big event before summer. With high school pausing for a few months, it felt like the perfect way to say goodbye to the grind of daily classes and hello to the endless possibilities of summer freedom.

When the night began to wind down and the guests started to leave, I lingered to say my goodbyes, soaking up the last bit of the evening's joy. I lived just around the corner and two city blocks away, it was a walk I could have done blindfolded. Despite it being well after midnight, I felt at ease in my neighborhood. My neighborhood was quiet and safe, the kind of place where people left their doors unlocked and everyone knew each other by name. I had walked that route more times than I could count, and I had never had a reason to feel unsafe.

But as I stepped onto the sidewalk away from the party lights that night, something about the air felt different. It was subtle at first, a strange, heavy stillness that seemed to press against my skin. The sounds I usually associated with my neighborhood were absent. No crickets chirping, no murmured conversations drifting from open windows, no hum of distant cars. Even the streetlights seemed dimmer than usual, casting weak halos of light that barely reached the ground.

I shook off the unease, convincing myself it was just my imagination playing tricks on me after such a lively evening. But a few minutes into my walk, I heard it. A faint, high-pitched squeaking sound coming from somewhere behind me. At first, I thought it was nothing a creaky gate or a loose bike chain. But the sound grew louder, steadier, until it was impossible to ignore.

When I turned to look, I saw an old pickup truck coming down the street. Its headlights were faint, its engine emitting a rhythmic squeal with every rotation of the engine's belt. I did not recognize the truck or its sound from the neighborhood. The driver slowed as he passed me, and for a moment, our eyes met. He smiled a thin, unsettling grin that made my stomach flip. His face was unfamiliar, and his presence felt wrong, out of place in a neighborhood where I knew everyone.

I forced a stiff smile of my own, trying to appear unbothered, and kept walking. The truck turned the corner, and relief washed over me as the squeaking sound faded into the distance. I told myself I was being paranoid. That man did not want anything to do with me. It's just a random driver. There is no reason to overreact.

But before I could fully convince myself, the squeaking noise returned, louder this time. My heart sank as I realized the truck had circled the block. The driver was back, moving slowly, scanning the street. I kept my eyes forward, pretending not to notice, but my mind was racing. The stretch of sidewalk I was on offered no cover, no trees, no parked cars, nothing to shield me from view. On this unusual night, there were no people on their front porches taking in the night air. I was painfully aware that meant no witnesses to whatever the man's intentions were. I knew at once I was in trouble.

I quickened my pace, keeping it subtle enough not to draw attention. I did not want to provoke him, did not want to give him a reason to escalate his plans. My plan was simple: get home as quickly as possible without making it obvious that I was afraid or aware of his presence. But there was a problem with my plan. I was at least a block and a half away from home. I was too far to turn back to the closed down party and too far away to run to my house.

The truck seemed to speed up as well, matching my pace then it disappeared around the corner.

This was my chance, and I took it. With the truck out of sight I bolted down the sidewalk. My heart nearly dropped when I heard the truck's squeaky, squawking return. The truck's third pass left no doubt in my mind. This was not random. He was looking for me. I had to think quickly. If it came down to a physical struggle I would be overpowered. If he saw me running, it could trigger the driver to react. I quickly decided if he thought I was unaware of his stalking, I might have a chance. I decided to use the cover of darkness and the trees to my advantage. I altered my stride from a casual walk to a sprint, and back to an unassuming walk whenever I came upon areas that concealed my position. By the time I reached the entrance to my block, I was almost running, the cover of the trees provided a small measure of relief. I ducked into the shadows, my breath coming in short, shallow bursts as I listened for the sound of the truck's engine. When it passed again, I saw the driver slowing, his eyes scanning the sidewalk where I should have been. Either he overshot his stop, or I outpaced his pursuit. It was just enough time for me to make a final break for it.

With the truck behind me, I sprinted the final stretch to my front door, my legs burning with effort, my ears straining for any sign of pursuit. The truck's engine squealed in the distance, and I knew I did not have much time. Fumbling with my keys, I finally managed to unlock the door and slam it shut behind me. I bolted the locks and slid the chain into place, collapsing against the door as my body shook with adrenaline.

Safe inside, the weight of what had just happened began to sink in. I had been followed, hunted like prey on streets I thought I knew so well. The same streets I had confidently walked many times before. If I had not made it home, if I had not been fast enough or cautious enough, what might have happened?

I did not tell anyone about that night. Fear and shame kept me silent. What if no one believed me? What if they blamed me for walking home alone? My mother would not let me go out again if she knew. I ran down a list of potential reactions of my family and friends. I feared the outcome of them all and did not tell anyone. For weeks, I lived with the memory of that man and his truck, the sound of its squeaking belt haunting my dreams. Every time I stepped outside, I felt the weight of his eyes on me, even though I had not seen him since.

Looking back, I regret my silence. My fear may have protected me in the moment, but it also allowed danger to linger in my neighborhood, unchecked and unchallenged. There were other girls, other kids who might have crossed paths with that man, and my decision to keep quiet could have put them at risk.

That night revealed more to me about fear and overcoming it than I could have imagined. Fear is powerful, but it thrives in isolation. It whispers lies, telling you that you are alone, that your strength is not enough. But the truth is, you are never truly alone. No matter how fierce the storm or how faint the trial, God is always present. He does not promise an easy escape, but as a loving Father, He walks with you, guiding you through every challenge, leading you toward His purpose for your life.

Even in my moment of panic, when fear clouded my mind and I did not have the presence of mind to call on His name, He was still there. In the midst of chaos, He gave me clarity. When fear sought to paralyze me, He granted me the wisdom and strength to find a way forward. I know without a doubt that the courage and logic I found in that moment were not my own. At just sixteen, I lacked the experience to navigate such a trial alone.

But God had a plan, one greater than the darkness that threatened me. Whatever evil was intended for me that night was no match for His purpose for my life. And because of Him, I walked away, not just unharmed, but with a testimony of His unwavering presence, His power, and His faithfulness.

The same unwavering presence that carried me through that night is available to you as well. No matter what fear whispers to you, no matter how dark or uncertain your path may seem, know this, God is with you. He is not distant or indifferent. He is right there in the midst of your situation, ready to guide, strengthen, and uphold you.

Fear wants to convince you that you are powerless, that you are alone, but that is a lie. You are never alone, and you never fight your battles on your own. The same God who spoke light into darkness, who calmed raging seas, who knew you before you were born, is walking beside you now. He sees what you cannot. He knows what you do not. And He has already prepared the way forward for you.

When fear grips your heart, when the weight of life feels too heavy to bear, call on Him. Even if you do not have the words, even if all you have is a whispered Jesus, He hears you. He has never abandoned you, and He never will. His plans for your life are greater than the obstacles before you, and no evil, no darkness, no fear is stronger than His purpose.

So, stand firm. When you feel weak, He is your strength. When you feel lost, He is your guide. Trust in Him, and you will see that fear has no power where your faith in Him resides. What was meant to steal, kill or destroy can become the very testimony that lifts, strengthens, and reminds you. You are never alone. Trust God.

Self Reflection

What specific situation in your past caused you to feel a strong fear of harm?

What signs did you notice in your body and mind when that fear took hold?

At the time, did you overestimate the danger, underestimate it, or see it clearly?

What short-term effects did fear have on your life right after the event?

What long-term patterns, beliefs, or habits came out of that experience?

Growth & Reflection

How has facing that fear prepared you to handle challenges today?

Did the experience shift how you see safety, courage, or resilience?

How do you use what you learned from that fear to support or guide others?

If you encountered a similar situation now, what would you do differently based on your growth?

THE BOOKS AND THEIR COVERS

Standing on the corner, waiting for the bus, I could not help but think there had to be a better way. Whoever designed this city's public transportation clearly did not rely on it. It was outdated, impractical, and never seemed to take into account the countless places people actually needed to go. But like it or not, I needed that bus. At sixteen, it was my ticket to freedom. It was a lifeline to my job at a nursing home that paid better than any minimum wage gig nearby. So, four or five days a week, I pushed aside my dislike for the city bus and climbed aboard.

Riding the bus was its own little world with unspoken rules. Just like the school bus, the safest place was near the driver. Not that the driver would necessarily protect you, but the front of the bus was generally occupied by elderly passengers who posed no threat. The back? That was reserved for the troublemakers, the people who could hold their own, and groups traveling together. Since I did not fit into any of those categories, I always headed for the front.

On this particular day, after paying my fare and finding a seat, I settled in for the ride, leaning my head against the window, hoping the trip would pass quickly. The usual noise filled the bus, harmless banter in the back, the hum of the engine, the quiet shuffling of passengers. But then I felt someone's eyes on me. I glanced across the aisle and was struck by a stunning young woman staring at me. For a moment, I was taken aback by her beauty. It was the kind of beauty that demanded attention, the kind that could stop time for the beholder.

And then her lips moved. She said my name. I was floored. "It's me, Stephanie," she said. Suddenly, it all clicked, this beautiful woman was my cousin! Years earlier, we had been in the same fourth grade class. Shortly after, life took us in different directions. My family moved to the other side of the city, and we lost touch. Somewhere along the way, puberty had been incredibly generous to Stephanie, while I was still waiting for my turn in the genetic lottery.

We caught up briefly, reminiscing about our childhood, and then her stop came. She gave me a radiant smile, and just like that, she was gone. Later that evening, I told my mom about our impromptu family reunion. I could not stop talking about how beautiful and put together Stephanie appeared. It was more than her beauty, she seemed to be on the path to success. Her speech, diction, attire, and confidence were all flawless. My internal dialogue ranged from questioning the validity of our relation to disbelief that we were the same age. My mom listened politely but seemed uninterested. "Good for her," she said with a hint of indifference. But I was amazed at the person Stephanie was growing up to become. I was convinced she was on the fast track to winning in life.

A few months later, the city bus delivered another unexpected reunion. I was at the bus transfer hub when I locked eyes with someone I could never forget. It was Anthony, my childhood friend and former crush. Time had been kind to him, too. Standing well over six feet tall with an athletic build, he looked more like an Adonis than Anthony. We had been friends as kids, though he was closer to my brother. After I moved, we lost touch. Now, here he was, all grown up, looking better than ever.

I was hoping for a quick conversation, perhaps a chance to exchange phone numbers and catch up. But instead, I fumbled badly. As I tried to approach him, I stepped right into a wad of gum. It got all over my shoe, and as I tried to scrape it off, I made it worse, getting it stuck to the other shoe. Anthony smiled at first, but as I struggled with the gum, his expression shifted to one of sympathy, or maybe pity. Mortified, I gave him a small wave and continued my failed attempt to clean my shoes. His bus arrived, and just like that, he was gone.

A few months later, I received a phone call that shattered my world. It was my brother, his voice heavy with the kind of sorrow you cannot prepare for. He had just seen a story on the evening news. It was news that left me reeling. Anthony, our friend, had been murdered by a rumored rival, while riding his bicycle not far from his home. The weight of those words hit me like a tidal wave, pulling me under a current of shock and disbelief. It seemed impossible to wrap my mind around it. How could Anthony be gone so quickly from a life he barely got to experience?

I kept replaying our last encounter over and over in my mind, grasping at the memory of him so vibrant, so full of energy, as if life was just beginning to unfold for him. I remembered wanting to approach him for what could have been our final conversation. Remembering the smirk he gave me when I last saw him made it even more difficult to realize Anthony was gone. As silly and superficial as it might seem, I could not help but think about the impossibility of it all. How could someone so young, attractive, and full of life be taken from us in such a callous and violent way? Anthony looked too good, too healthy, for death. But now he was gone. The finality of it was a crushing realization. About a year after the news of Anthony's death, my mother unexpectedly brought up Stephanie's name in conversation. The mention of her took me back to that brief, chance meeting we had on the bus not long before. I vividly remembered how she had looked that day. She was so full of life, so radiant, her energy almost palpable. I told my mom about that encounter, recalling how vibrant and beautiful Stephanie had appeared, as if nothing could touch her.

But then my mom quietly dropped a bombshell that left me speechless. Stephanie had passed away from AIDS. The words hung in the air, impossible to grasp. How could it be? The last time I had seen her, she seemed so alive, so untouched by anything that could hint at such a devastating reality. And yet, just like Anthony, she was gone. She was another life snuffed out far too soon, another person who seemed invincible in my mind, only to be taken away by something beyond comprehension.

Both Stephanie and Anthony, with their stunning looks and magnetic presence, seemed to embody the qualities that society so often glorifies. Stephanie had grown into this strikingly beautiful woman, the kind of person who turned heads effortlessly, while
Anthony had the full package, he was kind, handsome, tall, athletic physique which all made him look like he was destined for success. To anyone on the outside, they had it all. They had what people associate with success, confidence, and an easy path in life.

So often, we place value on these external qualities, as though beauty, strength, and the appearance of success are the tickets to a fulfilled life. But beneath those polished surfaces, they both carried burdens and faced struggles no one could see. Their outward appearances told a story that was not entirely true, a reminder that the things society favors are not always what leads to lasting happiness or a meaningful existence.

These two losses were hard to recover from. Life, I realized, is so fragile and unpredictable. One moment, someone is standing before you, full of life and promise, and the next, they are gone, leaving behind nothing but memories. I found myself asking questions I could not answer. Why them? Why not me? What was it about their paths that led to such tragic ends?

In the midst of my grief and confusion, I began to see life through a different lens. It became clear that life is not about comparing our journey to someone else's, nor is it about measuring who has the smoother road or who bears the heavier burden. Each of us is on a path uniquely our own, with its own twists, turns, and lessons that no one else can fully understand or experience. We often look at others and think we know their story, but the truth is, we never really know the weight

someone else is carrying, just as they can never truly know ours. Reflecting on the lives of Stephanie and Anthony, both tragically cut short, I learned a powerful lesson: never judge a book by its cover. On the surface, they both seemed vibrant, full of life, untouched by anything that could bring them down. But beneath that surface was a reality I could not see. There was a silent battle neither of them deserved to fight. Their struggles, though hidden, were real and profound. It made me realize that everyone's life, no matter how perfect it may appear from the outside, has layers of unseen complexity and hardship.

This understanding brought with it a deeper lesson about life. We often fall into the trap of looking at others and feeling envious or frustrated by their apparent ease or good fortune. We imagine their lives to be without struggle simply because we cannot see the storms, they are weathering. But life is not about walking someone else's path, it is about walking your own with grace, strength, and faith. What looks like a smooth road for one person may be fraught with hidden struggles, and what feels like an impossible path for us may be leading us exactly where we are meant to be.

In the end, it is not about how our journey compares to someone else's. It is about embracing the road we are on, trusting that every twist and turn has its purpose. The future holds different possibilities for each of us, and while we may not always understand the reasons behind the challenges we face, we can trust that our journey is shaping us into who we are meant to become. Contentment is not obtained through comparison, but by recognizing the beauty of our own story, in all its complexity and imperfection. Every path, no matter how difficult, holds lessons meant for us alone, and that is where the true value of life lies.

Self Reflection

What situation, opportunity, or relationship first appeared attractive or beneficial to you?

What qualities or appearances made it seem good at the time?

What truths eventually came to light that contradicted your first impression?

What consequences, positive or negative, came from engaging in this situation?

Did you ignore your intuition or inner voice along the way?

Growth & Reflection

What did this experience teach you about discernment and looking deeper than appearances?

How has it changed the way you evaluate people, opportunities, or decisions?

Are there any lessons learned to make future choices that align with deeper truth, not just surface appearances?

THE GRACE DESERVED

Back-to-school shopping was an event in my household that was eagerly anticipated. For my mom, a single mother juggling finances while trying to give us the best she could, it was a serious mission. She and her friends would scour every store, flipping through racks and shelves in search of the best deals on clothes for us kids. I realize now, looking back, just how much effort she put into this seemingly mundane task. She did not have much for herself, but she always ensured we were well-fed, clean, and dressed in nice clothes, even if they were not the latest styles or brand names that other kids had.

The year I started fourth grade, I hit a growth spurt that left me towering over my classmates. I had always been tall for my age, but suddenly, I was taller than my teacher, and to make things worse, my feet had also grown larger, much larger than most of the other kids. This awkward phase of rapid growth left me feeling self-conscious,

especially when I saw my reflection, gangly and out of place. That year, I was hoping, more than anything, for a pair of new sneakers. Sneakers, to me, meant fitting in, being just like everyone else. So, when my brothers and I piled into the car for our annual back-to-school shopping trip, I was filled with anticipation. I was thrilled when we pulled up to an athletic store, convinced
that this was finally the year I would get my coveted sneakers. But my excitement quickly faded. It became clear that this stop was not for me; it was for my brothers. They were getting new shoes, and I was left wandering aimlessly through the aisles, my heart sinking deeper with each step. It felt like my hope was being teased, so close, yet out of reach.

When we finally got back in the car, I held out hope that maybe the next stop would be for me. But my heart sank further when we pulled up to a familiar place, Hofheimer's. I recognized it at once, not even needing to see the sign. Hofheimer's was the store we visited every single year, and I dreaded it. I had been dragged there countless times before, knowing full and well what awaited me in the dimly lit basement, a pair of black-and-white dress shoes. They were the same style I had been forced to wear for years. I groaned and protested, begging my mom for something, anything, other than those shoes, but my efforts were futile. The outcome was inevitable. My mom, determined as ever, bought me those black-and-white shoes once again.

I could not understand it at the time. Why did my brothers get the sneakers I so desperately wanted while I was left with dress shoes I hated? Why couldn't she just get me the shoes that would help me blend in with everyone else, the shoes that would make me feel normal? I felt overlooked, misunderstood, and a little resentful. But years later, I would discover there was so much more to those shoes than I could have ever imagined.

One day, in casual conversation, my mom brought up our back- to-school shopping trips. She mentioned Hofheimer's with a fondness that surprised me. I could not help laughing and asking, "Why on earth would you miss dragging me into that dingy basement to buy ugly shoes?" To my surprise, she looked at me with a serious expression and said, "Because I can." Her words hung in the air for a moment before she told me a story I had never heard before.

My mother grew up in the 1950s, during a time when segregation and racism were still very much alive in this country. When she was a child, my grandmother would take her and her brothers downtown to buy shoes. Hofheimer's was considered the best shoe store in the city, but my mom and her siblings were not allowed inside. Back then, black people were forbidden from trying on shoes that white customers might purchase. Instead, they had to wait outside on the sidewalk. A store employee would come out with a piece of paper, have my grandmother trace my mother's feet, and then return inside to fetch a pair of shoes that neither my mom nor my grandmother had any say in. No trying them on, no selecting the style or color, just pay and go. My mother never even set foot in the store.

Hearing this story for the first time was a revelation. I had grown up in a world where she and I could walk into any store and try on any shoes of our choosing. I knew nothing of the discrimination and injustice my mom had faced. Suddenly, everything made sense. My mom's insistence on taking us to Hofheimer's every year wasn't just about buying shoes, it was about something far deeper. She insisted that I try a size up, a size down, and found the pair that fit just right regardless of how many pairs of shoes it took. It was not about making sure the shoes fit, it was about exercising a freedom she never had as a child. It was about reclaiming a right that had been denied to her as a child. The simple act of walking into that store and having me try on shoes was her victory. It was a way of healing the wounds of her past and ensuring that her children would never face the same indignities she had suffered.

That memory of me groaning and sulking as she made me try on pair after pair was no longer just about a pair of ugly shoes. It was about resilience, about the progress that comes from fighting against injustice and standing tall in the face of it. It was about healing from the trauma of discrimination and humiliation inflicted upon mother and child. It was about the irony of the very store that shunned my mother, still being in business decades later when our lives paralleled. My brothers, with their wild energy and refusal to wear anything but sneakers, were spared from this ritual. But I, who could be trusted to behave in a dress wearing those ugly shoes, became the symbol of her triumph.

Today, I look back on those shoes with a new sense of pride. What I once saw as a burden, I now recognize as a powerful expression of my mother's love, strength, and determination. She had taken her pain and turned it into something beautiful. It became an opportunity for her children to have what she never did. She made sure we knew our worth and that we could walk into any store, try on anything we wanted, without feeling the rejection of being denied.

Even though times have changed, that memory stays with me. It serves as a constant reminder of the progress we have made as a family, as a community, and as individuals. It also reminds me of the sacrifices she made and the many quiet victories she claimed along the way. Although I will never fully know or understand many of those battles, I know this one.

Today, when I reflect on those back-to-school shopping trips, I see them through a lens of deep gratitude. What I once viewed as disappointments were actually acts of love, resilience, and silent rebellion against the injustices my mom and others had faced. The shoes she chose for me were not just about appearances. They carried with them the weight of her experiences, her triumphs, and her fierce determination to give her children the dignity she had been denied.

In the same way, many of the decisions our parents make, whether they seem trivial or frustrating to us, often carry deeper meanings we might not understand in the moment. My mom did the best she could with what she had, and that is all any parent can do. We forget, sometimes, that they are not just parents but people. People with their own histories, battles, and struggles. They may not always get it right, but they are fighting for us in ways we may never fully understand.

Parents deserve grace for the paths they navigated before and with us. Often parents must navigate uncharted waters, balancing their own issues while striving to give their child a life. Often their desires are to give a better life than they had. Their choices, whether seen as mistakes or triumphs, are woven from the threads of love and hope, even when we cannot see it. In giving our parents grace, we not only acknowledge their humanity but also create space for deeper connection, healing, and gratitude in the shared story of our lives.

Self Reflection

What do you know about your parents' childhoods, and how might those experiences have shaped who they became?

What struggles, hardships, or sacrifices did your parents face before they became parents?

In what ways might they have been doing the best they knew how, even if it wasn't perfect?

How might their unhealed wounds or limitations have influenced how they showed up as parents?

If you imagine your parents as young adults with dreams and fears of their own, how does that change the way you see them now?

How can giving grace to your parents free you from repeating cycles of bitterness or blame?

Growth & Reflection

In what ways have you unconsciously inherited both strengths and struggles from your parents?

How can you honor the lessons they gave you without carrying forward their pain?

Where can you choose to grow differently to break cycles they couldn't?

How can shifting perspective from blame to understanding change how you live your own life?

What kind of legacy do you want to create for the next generation that reflects both grace and growth?

THE INTENTIONS OF OTHERS

Being the new kid at school is tough. But being the new kid every single year during elementary school? That is a whole different level of torture. Imagine the dread of walking into a classroom mid-year, not knowing anyone, and having to find your place all over again. Each time I was forced to start over, it felt like climbing a mountain that grew steeper and more treacherous with each attempt. Despite my good grades and polite demeanor, I began to feel a deep-seated disdain for school. It was not the homework or the early mornings, it was the loneliness and constant uncertainty. Just as I was ready to give up hope, I met Connor.

Connor was that kid. The kid everyone in school knew about, and not in a good way. He was a constant source of chaos and disruption in the classroom. His desk was not in the middle of the room like the rest of ours. Instead, it was placed right next to the teacher's desk. It was if he were a ticking time bomb that needed constant surveillance. Sometimes he was more of a storm the teacher needed to shield the rest of us from.

If there was something mischievous to be done, you could bet Connor had already tried it. Playing trash can basketball with crumpled-up assignments in the middle of a lesson? That was Connor. Talking over the teacher while she struggled to keep the class focused? Yep, that was him too. He was notorious for kicking chairs, hitting classmates, and outright ignoring any assignment given to him. He was a whirlwind of chaos wrapped in a child's body, and no one knew how to contain him.

Our teacher, a patient woman by nature, seemed to be reaching the end of her rope. The usual punishments did not work on Connor. Sending him to the principal's office was a mere inconvenience, and time-outs in the corner were just another stage for his antics. I remember one day when he turned his time-out punishment into an impromptu dance routine. His exaggerated facial expressions made the whole class giggle, much to our teacher's frustration. Nothing seemed to deter him, and every day was a battle to keep the class under control. Then, in a moment of sheer exasperation, our teacher reached for her final card, calling Connor's mom.

Any other kid would have immediately sat up straight with a look of fear in their eyes. But not Connor. He grinned, a devilish sparkle in his eye, daring the teacher to follow through. With all of us watching in tense silence, the teacher marched to the office and made the phone call. We all assumed Connor was about to face some major consequences when he got home. But we were in for a surprise. His mom had a different plan.

The next day, the atmosphere in the classroom was different. Our teacher seemed unusually calm, as if she knew something the rest of us did not. She checked the classroom clock a few times and insisted that we stay on schedule. As soon as Connor started his usual antics, she did not raise her voice or send him out. Instead, she told the class to gather around on the rectangle carpet which was usually reserved for story time. As instructed, we formed a horseshoe around the front of the room. With a stern look, she announced that it was time for a special guest and that we were to be on our very best behavior.

The door creaked open, and in walked Connor's mom with a stern expression on her face and a belt in her hand. The room fell silent, our eyes widening in shock. Connor, who had been so fearless before, suddenly looked terrified. His mom stormed in, her voice booming, announcing that she was there to show Connor what happened when he misbehaved. Our teacher, now emboldened, ordered us to sit quietly and watch, warning that anyone who laughed or looked away would be next. She even threatened to call our mothers if we did not behave.

We sat there, frozen with fear and confusion, as Connor's mom proceeded to whip him in front of the entire class. She spun him around in circles inside the horseshoe of children, as he tried to escape the belt. His cries of pain filled the room. The sharp crack of the belt against his skin and his wailing is a sound I will never forget. I had only been at that school for a few weeks, and I could not believe what I was seeing.

I wanted to run back to my old school, to a place where things made sense. A place where my classmates were never publicly whipped in class. I did not understand why we were forced to witness our classmates' brutal beating. I could not help but think, was this a truly a threat to keep the rest of us in line or was it something more sinister? Were we unknowingly pawns turned accomplices to Connor's beating and humiliation? Either way it was something no child on either side of the scenario should be forced to endure.

When it was over, Connor's mother signed him out of school and took him home. His light-skinned body was marred with red colored welts. His sobs echoed down the hallway as they left. Internally I wanted to sob too. The classroom was silent as the shock on our faces testified on our behalf. Our teacher, looking somewhat justified, tried to explain why it needed to happen, but her words did not reach us. In my mind she was the crazy lady that literally forced us to watch that horrible scene. When no one moved or made a sound our teacher yelled recess as if it were the solution. We were sent outside as if playing on the monkey bars or the swings could erase what we had just witnessed. For me it was pointless, the images of what I had seen burned into my mind.

Connor did not deserve that. Sure, he was a troublemaker, but no child deserves to be beaten and humiliated in front of their peers. When he returned to school a few days later, it was as if nothing had changed. He was still the same mischievous kid, still up to his old tricks. It became clear to me then that Connor's issues ran much deeper than what we saw in the classroom.

The public whipping had done something to spark a change in school operations. Whispers and rumors about the incident quickly spread through the school. An uproar was created among parents, leading to a new rule that banned any form of parental discipline on school grounds. Parents were no longer allowed in the classroom during school lessons. Despite all the poor choices that were made, our teacher kept her job and Connor kept being Connor. Thankfully, we did not see the return of his mother or her belt for the remainder of the school year.

Years went by, and life slowly stabilized for me. I finally managed to stay in one school long enough to feel like I belonged. By the time middle school came around, I ran into Connor again. He was different now. He was quieter, more withdrawn, as if the spark that once defined him had been dimmed. In high school, he became even more disconnected, almost like a shadow passing through the hallways, uninterested in school, and seemingly indifferent to everything but the streets.

By our sophomore year, Connor was gone. Connor had gotten mixed up in a life far from the classroom where he belonged. Connor dropped out of school and got involved with the wrong crowd. It did not take long before his life was cut short by crime in the very streets he clung to. Tragically, Connor was fatally shot during what should have been his senior year in high school.

The news of his murder quickly spread through the neighborhood as the police searched for a suspect. I could not help but think back to that chubby-faced boy from elementary school. He was the boy who made us laugh even when he should not have. He was also the kid who never quite fit in but did not seem to care. That boy died far too young, still just a kid in many ways, and I could not shake the feeling that maybe things could have been different for him.

As an adult now, with children of my own, I find myself reflecting on that day more often than I would like to admit. I understand now that Connor's mom was probably at her wit's end. She was tired and desperate, likely doing what she thought was best based on her own experiences growing up. In her own twisted way, her intentions were good although her actions were every bit wrong. That day in elementary school should have been handled differently. That day could have resulted in a different outcome if only one of the two adults present had fully thought about the consequences before the actions. What I witnessed did not teach me about discipline or about the importance of good behavior. That day taught me that good intentions, even in the care of trusted adults, can lead to terrible mistakes.

There are valuable lessons to be learned from watching someone get it wrong. Bad choices do not have to be passed down like some twisted heirloom. As children, we learn the difference between right and wrong. As adults, it is our job to apply that knowledge thoughtfully and wisely and make good decisions that render good outcomes. That day in school provided a live illustration of how the road to hell can indeed be paved with good intentions.

Connor's story stays with me, a haunting reminder that our actions create ripples, affecting others in ways we might never understand. One-size-fits-all solutions do not work because we are all complex, uniquely wired individuals. There is no substitution for patience, kindness, joy, peace, love, goodness, gentleness, self control, and love. We should all seek to practice more of each one every day. Even the slightest measure of any of those virtues could have made a difference that day and possibly in Connor's overall life. Connor's life may have been a short one, but it is one that affected mine. Remembering that day pushes me to question decisions, challenge the status quo, and encourage those around me to do the same. I chose to carry the lessons from Connor with me every day as a parent, a friend, and a human being trying to navigate this world with a little more understanding and a lot more compassion. I challenge you to do the same.

Self Reflection

Have you experienced a situation where a person's intentions differed from the impact of their actions?

Were there assumptions the other person made about you that didn't match your reality?

Have you ever had good intentions in your actions that resulted in unintended consequences for yourself or others? What could you have done differently in that situation?

Growth & Reflection

How did your actions, despite your intentions, impact the other person emotionally or practically?

Did you listen actively enough, or did you prioritize your idea of "help" over their autonomy? If not, what can you do differently in the future?

How can you use communication in future situations to align your good intentions with a better expected outcome for all people involved?

THE INSECURITIES

We did it! We finally moved up, not to the east side or some deluxe apartment in the sky, but into the heart of suburbia. Nestled in the neighborhood of our dreams was our new home. Our new place was not just a house. It was a beacon of hope for a brighter future, a place where our children could thrive in a top-notch school system and seize opportunities we could only have dreamed of. Sure, the houses were big, the lawns perfectly manicured, and the backyards sprawling, but it was more than that. It was the promise of a better life that had us packing up the U-Haul and setting off on this adventure. Before we knew it, we were unpacked, our boxes scattered like memories across our new home, each item finding its place as if it had been waiting for this moment all along. It did not take long for us to start meeting our new neighbors.

The very day we moved in, my husband was already chatting with a few of them outside, trading introductions and pleasantries. We soon realized we had forgotten some of the basic essentials. We needed to find the nearest store. As my husband was talking with one of the guys, I called out and asked him to pick up a few essentials. The neighbor quickly rattled off directions: take the main road to the flashing light, turn right, go to the stop sign, and then take a left. It seemed straightforward enough, but as fate would have it, we got lost. After a good laugh at our expense and a few extra wrong turns, we sheepishly returned to the neighbor, ready for round two of directions. This time, his wife Tina stepped in. She gave us precise step-by-step instructions that guided us there and back without a hitch.

    A week into our new life, I went to register our daughter at the local elementary school, excited for her to start this new chapter. As luck would have it, I ran into Tina again, along with another neighbor named Diane. They were chatting near the entrance, and when they saw me, they waved me over with friendly smiles. We exchanged a few words, and they seemed genuinely warm and welcoming. Tina even offered to introduce me to more of the women in the neighborhood, which I thought was incredibly kind. Just as I was starting to feel at ease, Diane leaned in with a smile and said, "You're really pretty."

For a moment, I felt flattered, a warm blush rising to my cheeks as I prepared to thank her for the compliment. But before I could get a word out, she added, "We'll have to keep our husbands away from you." Her words hung in the air like an awkward, unexpected backhand to the face. I blinked, trying to process the comment. Was she joking? It did not seem like it. There was not the slightest hint of a smile on her face. I forced a laugh, trying to lighten the mood. "I don't want your husbands, I have my own!" I said with a smile, hoping to smooth things over. But Diane did not relent. "Yeah, well, you're still too pretty to be around our men," she said, turning on her heel and walking away, leaving me standing there in a state of stunned disbelief.

I had never encountered anything like that before. I was caught somewhere between being offended and oddly appreciative of her blunt honesty. On the surface, Diane's comment felt like a slap, a judgment of my character based on nothing but her own assumptions. She did not know me, had not bothered to learn who I was, and seemed to have already made up her mind about me and my character. But as I stood there, trying to shake off the sting of her words, I realized there was something raw and strangely honest about what she had said. Once I moved past the initial shock, I found myself appreciating her candor, even if it was wrapped in a layer of rudeness. In her own way, Diane had saved me from trying to build a friendship that should never be. She spared me from investing myself into someone whose own insecurities would sabotage any semblance of friendship.

I could not help but wonder what had prompted Diane's reaction. Was she speaking from a place of past betrayal, a wound still raw from some old scar? Was it insecurity that drove her? Was it a fear born from experiences that I could not begin to understand? Or was this a learned behavior, passed down through generations as a misguided way to protect herself from potential pain? I realized I might never know her story, but there was still a lesson in her actions. Fear and insecurity are powerful emotions, often intertwining and feeding off each other, fueling behaviors that can be hurtful and defensive.

Diane's bluntness, while off-putting, held an unexpected lesson: sometimes, the harshest hearts are the best teachers in disguise. Her words made me reflect deeply on relationships, fear, and trust. They reminded me that the walls people build around themselves are often constructed out of pain and vulnerability, not malice. I did not take Diane's comments personally. There was no need to. I knew perfectly well where my morals and values came from. I also knew that attractiveness did not equate to adultery or the treat there of. Diane had formed fear or insecurity in her marriage from an issue that did not involve me.

For any woman or man grappling with fear or insecurity in their marriage, remember the foundation marriage is built upon. Larger than your affections and intentions towards your spouse, there is a greater foundation. Marriage is also more than a legal contract between two people. It is a sacred covenant, a bond that involves not just the couple but also God. When you exchanged vows, you made a promise not just to each other, but to God Himself. If you are ever facing struggles, that is where you should turn first to Him. Remember, when you committed yourself to marriage, you were not alone in that commitment. God took ownership too, promising to uphold and protect the bond you created together.

This understanding will bring a profound sense of peace. You do not have to feel like you are fighting alone to protect a marriage because it is not yours alone. If you genuinely believe in God's almighty power and unwavering truth, then why wouldn't you want Him as the guardian of your marriage and your heart? He is more capable, more steadfast, and more loving than any human could ever be.

Whatever adversities you may face, trust Him to deliver you through it all. God does not break promises, and He will not be mocked. This is not something to take lightly. He will defend and honor the covenant you made with Him, standing by it more faithfully than you or your spouse ever could. Trust in His strength and His plan, knowing that even if others let you down, God never will. He is always there, ready to guide you, protect you, and bring justice where it is due.

For those who believe they can interfere with a marriage blessed by God, they do not yet understand what they are up against. They may try to sow doubt or discord, but in the end, it is always God who has the final word. You are His child, His creation. You are deeply loved and cared for beyond measure. When you embrace the power of His love, stand on His promises, and place your trust in Him, you will realize that this marriage is not just yours, it is His. And with God at the center, there is nothing to fear.

As I step into this new chapter of life, I have come to understand that trust and faith are not just ideals. They are the foundation of a strong and lasting relationship. Trust in your partner cultivates honesty and vulnerability, allowing love to flourish without fear. Trusting in yourself gives you the courage to communicate, to forgive, and to grow, even when challenges arise. But above all, trust in God is what elevates a marriage beyond human effort, it becomes a sacred union, guarded by a love far greater than any imperfection or doubt.

God's role in marriage is not merely ceremonial, it is central. When you invite Him into your marriage, you are not just asking for
blessings. You acknowledge that this bond is sacred and worthy of His guidance and protection. His presence elevates every moment, reminding you that the love you share is part of a greater plan. With God at the center, your marriage gains a strength that transcends the trials of life. No argument, no financial strain, no external threat can break what He has ordained, as long as you stay faithful to your covenant and to Him.

This trust in God is not passive, it is an active choice, made daily. It means surrendering your worries, insecurities, and doubts to Him, trusting that He will carry you through even the darkest days. It means turning to Him not just in moments of crisis, but in times of joy and gratitude, recognizing that every blessing comes from His hand. It means praying together as a couple, seeking His wisdom in your decisions, and relying on His strength when yours falters. Through this daily practice of faith, you weave spiritual resilience into your marriage that no earthly challenge can unravel.

When you face trials, and you will, this trust becomes your greatest weapon and shield. You will find that fear has no power over you because you are anchored in a truth that cannot be altered. That truth is God's love for you and His commitment to the covenant you made. Even when doubts arise, even when the world seems intent on testing your bond, you can stand firm, knowing that you are not fighting alone. God is the steady force working on your behalf, orchestrating solutions, offering peace, and strengthening your resolve.

Living in this trust does not mean ignoring challenges or pretending that problems do not exist. On the contrary, it means facing them with courage and clarity, knowing that you are equipped to overcome them. It means loving your spouse with an open heart, even when it is difficult, because your love is grounded in something eternal. It means forgiving mistakes, because you recognize that grace is the glue that holds a marriage together. And it means extending that same grace to yourself, understanding that growth is a journey and that God's love for you is unwavering, even in your own imperfections.

Finally, trust in God brings with it a profound sense of freedom. You no longer need to carry the weight of every worry, every fear, or every "what if" on your own shoulders. You can release it all to Him, knowing that He is more than capable of handling what you cannot. This freedom allows you to live boldly and love fearlessly, without the shadow of insecurity clouding your joy. It reminds you that your marriage is not just a partnership between two people, but a divine collaboration, guided by God.

So, as you navigate the twists and turns of life together, hold tightly to the truth. When you place your marriage in His hands, you are not just building a life together, you are building a legacy. That legacy will stand as a testament to His power and your devotion. With that combination, your marriage will not only survive the storms, but it will also break through them, becoming a beacon of inspiration for all who witness it.

Self Reflection

Is there a specific fear you have about the security of your relationship? If so, what is it?

What makes you feel confident and secure in your relationship with your partner? Is there anything you can do to increase or encourage growth in those areas?

Do you have specific feelings that arise when you think about the possibility of infidelity? Is it fear, anger, sadness, or something else?

How much of your fear comes from past wounds like childhood, past relationships, or betrayals, versus your partner's current actions?

Growth & Reflection

How would your relationship feel different if you trusted yourself more deeply, regardless of your partner's actions?

What can you do to lessen and eventually remove those fears?

What small steps can you take today either in prayer, communication, self-care, or mindset, that would move you closer to peace within your relationship?

THE HELPING HANDS

It was like discovering a bird with a broken wing. I did not know exactly how to help her, but I knew I had to at least try. Cindy lived in the apartment right above us. Like my husband and me, she was in her early twenties, a new parent, navigating life with a one-year-old. Cindy and her boyfriend had moved in a few months after us, keeping to themselves, which I completely understood. Living in an apartment complex means proximity you did not necessarily choose, so guarding your personal space made sense.

My husband and I were both working, so it took a while before we noticed that something seemed off in the apartment above us. I initially shrugged it off, thinking I was imagining things. After hearing strange noises one too many times, I confided in my husband that something wasn't right. We tossed around a few theories about what could be going on upstairs, but none of them seemed to fit.

So, we let it go. For a short while the noise stopped altogether.

That summer, my brother came to stay with us. I decided to switch shifts at work to make the most of the time we had together. We had not lived in the same place for years, so I wanted to take advantage of every moment I could spend with my brother. One lazy afternoon, we were sitting in the living room with the TV on, just relaxing like we often did. That is when I heard it again. It was a faint, distant noise from above. At first, I thought I might be imagining it, but soon, it grew louder and more distinct. This time, it was unmistakable. The commotion upstairs was more than a faint noise. As I listened more intently it became clear the people upstairs were arguing. This was no ordinary argument. It was sharper, more aggressive, and filled with intensity.

I glanced at my brother, and in that instant, without a word spoken between us, we both knew exactly what was happening. There was a steady stream of loud commotions followed by a strange thud. The realization was chilling. Cindy, our upstairs neighbor, was being beaten, and this time, the sounds were more intense than anything I had ever heard from upstairs.

My brother did not hesitate. He jumped up, grabbed a broom, and started pounding on the ceiling with it, shouting at the people above to stop. His voice echoed through the apartment, but instead of calming things down, it only seemed to fuel the chaos. The sounds from above escalated as heavy footsteps thudded across the floor, followed by the terrifying noises of a chase, more screams, and the brutal impact of violence. Each crash felt like it reverberated through the walls. It was painfully clear that Cindy's boyfriend was beating her with a cruelty that we could hear but not see.

I rushed to grab my phone, dialing 911 with shaking hands as my brother and I stood frozen, straining to track every sound from above. The helplessness was overwhelming. No matter how many times we banged on the ceiling or yelled for them to stop, the violence continued. It was as though we were invisible bystanders to something horrific.

Then, suddenly, we heard the front door upstairs slam with a force that rattled the walls. Heavy footsteps pounded down the stairs. I ran to the window, heart racing, fully expecting to see Cindy fleeing for her life, desperate to escape the nightmare. But when I peeked out the window, my heart sank. It was not Cindy running, it was her boyfriend, storming out with fury in his every step. And behind him was Cindy, battered and bruised, with her clothes torn, her lip bleeding, and yet, in a scene that defied all logic, she was chasing after him pleading.

Her voice was desperate, pleading, as she begged him not to leave. The image of her once bright, vibrant self now reduced to this was seared into my mind. I could not reconcile the person I was acquainted with as the woman now in front of me, so wounded, physically, and emotionally. All the while she was still pleading with the very person who had caused her harm.

By the time the police arrived, Cindy had composed herself. She had wiped the blood from her lip, straightened her torn clothes, and in a tone that seemed almost rehearsed, she told them it had all been a misunderstanding. To our disbelief, several neighbors had called the police, just like we had, but even with all the concern around her, Cindy stuck to her story. Everything was fine, she insisted. She was okay.

Once the officers left, we were left with a sinking feeling in our chests, knowing this would not be the last time. And it was not. In the months that followed, the beatings became almost routine. The sounds of violence from above would start, we would call the police, and

Cindy would deny everything when they arrived. It was a vicious, heartbreaking cycle. Her boyfriend would attack, the police would intervene, and Cindy, trapped in her own cycle of fear and denial, would lie to protect him. Over time, the calls to the police grew less frequent. Her boyfriend had grown more careful, more calculating, learning to time his assaults perfectly so he could slip away just before the police arrived.

Then came the night that changed everything. This time, the noises from upstairs were worse than anything we had heard before. We could hear glass shattering, and the baby crying. Cindy's voice was raised in a way we had not heard before. She was fighting back. Her boyfriend's voice was dripping with rage, berating her for daring to defend herself. Outside, my neighbors and I gathered, nervous and unsure of what to do, our voices hushed as we debated how to intervene. I grabbed my phone once again, heart pounding, and called the police, fearing this time the violence might end in something even worse than before.

Minutes later, we watched as Cindy's boyfriend finally emerged from the apartment. This time, something was different. His shirt was stained with blood, and he looked disheveled, angrier than usual. For the first time since the beatings had begun, Cindy did not run after him. She did not chase him down the stairs or beg him to stay. She stayed behind, and we feared what we might find.

When the police arrived, they discovered Cindy in a state that
no lie or denial could cover. She was bloodied, bruised, and broken, and this time, there was no denying the abuse. For the first time, Cindy pressed charges. The police located her boyfriend and took him away. She was rushed to the hospital, and thankfully, her baby, their baby, was unharmed.

That night marked the end of a tragic chapter in Cindy's life that had unfolded right above our heads. But it also marked the beginning of a new chapter, one where she no longer had to hide her pain or protect the man who had caused it. I and the other neighbors had doubts if Cindy's resolve would hold. Months of trying to save Cindy in vain from her abuser left us with a sliver of hope that it was truly the last time. Honestly, I did not know how much more violence her body could withstand.

A week later, I saw her boyfriend return, this time under quite different circumstances. He came back with a police escort, two officers flanking him as he entered the building to gather the last of his things. It felt surreal, watching him move about under the watchful eyes of the law, knowing that this time, he had no control over the situation. Cindy stood outside her door, her protective order in hand, watching with a quiet strength that had not been there before. She did not flinch, did not speak, just watched as he hurriedly collected his belongings. For once, she was in control, and he could not intimidate her. It was clear to me that this was a turning point. It was a pivotal moment where she was reclaiming her life, her space, her dignity.

Once he was gone, Cindy knocked on my door. There was something different about her. She asked me, somewhat shyly, if the retail store I managed was hiring. Her voice wavered slightly as she explained her situation. She was now a single mother, needing a job to support herself and her child. Knowing that I knew more about her circumstances than she would have preferred must have been difficult. It must have taken a lot for her to ask me for anything. There was a vulnerability in her words, but also a quiet resolve. I could tell she was ready to try and build a new life, and this was the first step.

Without hesitation, I told her we were indeed hiring, and I encouraged her to apply. I wanted to help her, to be part of her journey to rebuild after all she had been through. When she applied, I fast tracked the process, hiring her on the spot. I scheduled her for training and made a point to pair her with some of my kindest, most supportive coworkers. I did not want her first day to feel overwhelming. After all it was her reentry into the working world. The ability to earn an income would help her regain her confidence. I even made sure to keep her first day light, carefully choosing tasks that would not put too much pressure on her.

When I checked in on her during her shift, she seemed good. There was a certain cheerfulness in her demeanor, a gratefulness for the opportunity. She gave me a friendly "hey girl" when I approached her work area and smiled. When I asked how things were going, Cindy told me she was happy to be working again and that she appreciated the chance to start over. It felt like a small but meaningful victory, like this could be the beginning of a new chapter for her, one where she was in control of her own life. Halfway into her shift, Cindy went on a 30-minute break.

Cindy never came back. She vanished. No goodbye, no explanation, just gone. The other employees and I theorized what could have happened to her. Perhaps she ran into her abusive ex, or she got a flat tire. Whatever it was we were helpless in helping her. We continued our shift and hoped for the best vowing to call the police if we did not hear from her. Since my shift was ending soon, I agreed to check if Cindy went back to her apartment above mine. Later that night, I noticed her car parked outside our apartment building. I could hear her footsteps overhead, as usual. She was home, but she had not come back to work. The pieces began to fall into place. It became obvious Cindy had quit without saying a word. At least she was safe and not a truly missing person. It was awkward and slightly comical that Cindy quietly quit on her first day and returned to her apartment above mine.

In a way, I was not entirely surprised. People quit jobs all the time. It's just the way the world works. Maybe she got a better offer while she was away. Maybe she just decided she was done. Either way, she didn't owe me an explanation. But then, a few days later, I spotted her in the parking lot. I figured she'd at least say something, offer a nod, a wave, anything. Instead, she looked right at me, then quickly ducked away, as if hoping I had not noticed.

And that's when it hit me: this was my first real lesson in why mixing business with personal relationships is rarely a good idea. For two weeks, she avoided me, making a deliberate effort to sidestep any interaction. Then, one afternoon, she finally approached. There was no hesitation in her step, no sign of discomfort, just a casual indifference.

She did not apologize for leaving without notice. Instead, she simply stated, matter-of-factly, that she hadn't liked the job. Retail, she explained, was dull, uninspiring, beneath her, even. So, she decided not to come back after her break. And even if she changed her mind, it would be difficult since she had thrown away her uniform.

And then, as if the thought had only just occurred to her, she spoke again. Her tone was flat, emotionless. She asked for her paycheck comprised of the two hours she had worked. It was not a request, nor even a demand. It was a transaction, a box to be checked, a minor inconvenience she was ready to put behind her. There was no arrogance in her voice, but no humility either. Just a cold, mechanical certainty, as if nothing about this exchange mattered in the slightest.

I stood there, stunned for a moment, processing what had just happened. Two hours. Two hours of work, and yet the effort she had put into those hours felt so minimal that there was no need to dodge me over quitting. Realizing that she only stopped dodging me to collect those two hours was another lesson for me.

In that moment, I realized that Cindy's journey was far more complicated than I had imagined. It was not just about finding a job or moving on from an abusive relationship. She was still trying to figure out who she was without him, without the chaos that had defined her life for so long. And perhaps, she was not quite ready to embrace the calm that came with independence. The job had been a lifeline, yes, but also a reminder of how far she had to go.

Perhaps Cindy had quit because the weight of her new reality was too much to bear all at once. The road ahead of her was going to be long and winding, filled with starts and stops, and I realized that my role in her story was not to fix things for her. All I could do was step aside and allow the chips to fall where they needed to settle. It was her life to live and figure out what she wanted. I silently hoped Cindy could find support when she was ready to take the next step.

Helping someone only works if they are ready to be helped. Cindy was not ready. She had not been ready when we called the police, and she was not ready when she started the job. She was still deep in her trauma, not yet aware of her own need to heal. It was not for me to fix, no matter how clear it seemed to me of what might help. I had to let go, no matter how unfortunate her circumstances were. It is a hard lesson, but one I learned: not all injustices are ours to right. Wisdom and discernment are needed to know when to step in and when to step back. Even when our hearts break for someone, we must recognize that healing is a deeply personal journey. Our role should be one of support and action when the time is right, trusting that God will handle the rest.

Self Reflection

What is your true motivation for wanting to help? Are you trying to fix, control, be needed, or genuinely support?

How do you recognize when someone isn't ready to receive help? What signs should you look for?

What is your boundary line between supporting someone and carrying what isn't yours to carry?

Are you comfortable with letting someone move at their own pace, even if it's slower than you want?

What steps can you take to prevent yourself from attaching your sense of success to whether others take your help?

Growth & Reflection

Have you tried asking the person in need of help if they would like your help before jumping in to assist with their problem?

Determine your current boundaries around helping such as "I can listen, but I won't take over their responsibilities" before stepping in with a potential solution.

What are some open ended questions you can ask yourself to gauge where the person in need is at mentally and emotionally to receiving help?

THE FLASHLIGHT CHURCH

Ah, milestone time! Eighteen years in the making and here we were, watching our little girl, our baby, about to graduate high school. Everything felt so surreal, so familiar, but with that twist of newness parenthood brings. Now, it was time to gear her up for her next big adventure, college. Yep, the leap into independence, self-discovery, and probably more laundry than she had ever done in her life.

With SAT scores already in the bag from junior year, college apps became the name of the game. We checked off boxes like pros. Essays, scholarships, mentorships, you name it, we were on it. The applications went out, and we just knew it was only a matter of time before her hard work paid off. By the second semester of her senior year, it felt like the payoff was just around the corner.

One afternoon she came home with an invitation from school for a mysterious yet prestigious award, yes, an actual award. Handed out by the school counselors, it came from a nonprofit group that promised a reward of "significant value." Intrigued, okay, maybe a little skeptical, I read that letter about a hundred times and drilled her with questions. A few of her friends with similar G.P.A.s got the same invite, so we figured, hey, it was legit. There was no phone number to RSVP, just a big push to attend, and a reminder for the graduates to wear their caps and gowns. Once I confirmed with the high school that it was a real ceremony, I circled the date on our calendars and got ready for the big day.

When the day arrived, we were practically buzzing with excitement and speculation. What could this "award of significant value" be? A scholarship? Cold, hard cash? A new laptop? Our imaginations ran wild. As we pulled up to the venue, an old Baptist church, we noticed something. There were different colored caps and gowns from all over the county. This was not just our high school, it was a multi-school event. The whole thing felt important. We squeezed into the overflow seating upstairs and got a bird's-eye view of the event. Down below, the graduates filed in, and I could not help but notice the table of white, gift-wrapped boxes next to the students' seating area. There had to be hundreds of them. The energy of the parental anticipation was palpable. I was not the only parent trying to X-ray those boxes with my eyes.

The service kicked off with organ music, students filed in, and the pastor welcomed everyone with a rousing sermon based on rap lyrics by musical artist J. Cole. It was not the direction I expected but I guess it was tailored for the multitude of young people in attendance. The ceremony was peppered with tributes and voting reminders for the upcoming election. After about an hour of ceremonies the passing of the collection plate, and a little bit of sermonizing, it was finally time for the awards. The anticipation was steadily building.

The three students who were church members went first. They each got $1,000 scholarships from the church, delivered in crisp white envelopes. The rest of us non-church member families exchanged nervous glances. If they were like me then they also did a quick headcount and math on the students in attendance that day. Of the graduates I could see from my seat, I counted a little over 300 students. I could not help ponder the budget or the benefactor of these three hundred plus gifts of significant value as detailed in the invitation letter. Then, they started calling the names of the non-member students. One by one, they walked across the stage according to their high school, collected their gift boxes, and returned to their seats.

From our perch above, I could not see inside the boxes, but I could definitely see the looks on the students' faces as they opened them. Let's just say... they did not look thrilled. My daughter shot me a look that said, "Mom, you're not going to believe this." I tried mouthing the words "what is it" but it was a fail. She simply shook her head and said nothing in return. After all the names were called, we rushed downstairs to meet her, hearts pounding, curiosity at its peak. Finally, I saw her. "What did you get?" I asked breathlessly. She handed me the box. I opened it, bracing for a tiny scholarship certificate or maybe a check... and pulled out a neon-colored plastic flashlight keychain.

Yes, you read that right. A flashlight keychain. At that moment, I was speechless. Not in awe, mind you, just baffled. My brain was working overtime to process what had just happened. An "award of significant value" had been hyped to the heavens, and this was it? A one- dollar keychain? Oh, the irony.

The mood outside was a stark contrast to the pre-ceremony excitement. Disappointment and confusion hung in the air like a cloud. My daughter, like the rest of the students, was over it. We all were. As parents, we felt duped, like we had bought into some elaborate bait-and-switch. But in the end, the joke was on us, but none of us were in a laughing mood. Days later the mood shifted as we jokingly referred to the experience as flashlight church. We discussed our disappointment with the ordeal and the role we played in it as well.

Had we approached that day with the right perspective, simply celebrating my daughter's academic achievements and appreciating the recognition, it would have been a moment of pure joy. Instead, our anticipation for something more clouded what was truly meaningful. We allowed the letter to set our expectations too high, falling into the trap of seeing only what we wanted to see, rather than recognizing the deeper purpose of the occasion. But in the end, that day did give us a gift, though not the one we expected. It offered us a lesson in humility, gratitude, and the importance of perspective. From that day, I promised myself not to allow money or financial gain to be a motivator for anything I do. When money is the motivator the purity of motive is exchanged for the money. The money can and will cloud all good judgment and decisions.

In my anticipation of my daughter receiving the promised gift of significant value, I was consciously generous in my contribution to the collection plate. In the moment I rationalized that since the church was giving my child and all the other students expensive gifts, then I should be generous in my giving. That was a huge lesson for me. As people, we should give solely to be generous and nothing more. Giving with the wrong motive always leads to disappointment and often resentment. I explained my errors to my children, ensuring they understood the valuable lessons and my mistakes from that day.

Years later, we still laugh about that little plastic keychain. It was not the scholarship we had imagined, but it turned out to be something far more valuable. It taught us a lesson that will last a lifetime: never let money or material rewards drive your decisions. We were so fixated on the potential worth of the award that we walked into that church blinded by our expectations.

Looking back, I realize there was significant value received that day. It was not in the contents of the gift box, but in the unintended wisdom gained. It was a reminder that life's greatest rewards often come wrapped in the unexpected. And for that, I am genuinely grateful to the flashlight church.

Self Reflection

When have you been drawn to something because of how it looked, only to later discover it wasn't what you imagined?

What qualities do you tend to notice first in people or situations, and how often do you dig beneath the surface?

Have you ever confused external success, charm, or status with deeper qualities like integrity, kindness, or resilience? How can you grow beyond that and look for those deeper qualities?

What past disappointments taught you to look beyond appearances before trusting, investing, or committing?

Growth & Reflection

What "shiny quality" do you personally present to the world, and does it align with who you truly are inside?

Are you currently pursuing something shiny that represents a substantial value, that may not bring lasting fulfillment?

How can you cultivate the patience to test and uncover what's genuine and truly valuable, rather than being caught up in appearances?

THE PAIN

If someone had told my younger self that by the age of twenty-one, I would be pregnant with my second child, I would have laughed. No, I would have outright dismissed such an absurd notion. Me? A mother of two before, most of my peers had even begun to navigate adulthood. Impossible. And yet, there I was, at that very age, carrying my second baby.

But despite the sheer surprise of it all, I was overjoyed. My husband and I were ready this time, or at least, we believed we were. We had everything we needed: our two-year-old's old baby accessories, a home already child-proofed, and most importantly, experience. We had braved the storm of first-time parenthood and come out the other side, wiser, stronger, and, we thought, better prepared for round two.

Just like the first time, months passed before I even realized I was pregnant. My genetics and tall frame concealed the growing life inside me, and pregnancy wasn't even a fleeting thought. But then, in an offhanded moment, my co-worker Dawn casually mentioned that she was expecting her fourth child. Her words struck something in me, a tiny spark of recognition that slowly unfurled into suspicion. Could it be? I rushed home, took a test, and there it was, confirmation. I was pregnant again.

From that moment, the planning began in earnest. Looking back, I sometimes wonder if a routine of monthly tests would have spared me the shock, given that I had no symptoms, no nausea, no outward signs of change. It was as if my body had hidden the secret from me. By the fifth month, my preparations kicked into high gear. My doctor had retired, so I sought a new physician, trusting a recommendation from a friend. But before I could even step foot into my appointment with the new physician, my world shifted in a way I never could have foreseen.

It started with a strange feeling. Not pain, not sickness, just an unsettling sense that something was... off. I was exhausted and drained, but the baby was fine. I could feel the reassuring flutters of life within me. That was all that mattered. I was scheduled to open the store that morning. I was the only manager on shift with keys. It was a short four- hour stretch, and I told myself I could push through. If I still felt unwell by the time my relief arrived, I would go home and rest. Simple.

With that plan in mind, I kissed my husband and toddler goodbye and headed to work. But the unease never faded. An hour into my shift, exhaustion clung to me like a dense fog. I tried to shake it off, grabbing a soft drink from the break room, sipping at it between assisting customers. The store was quiet, just a handful of shoppers, off-duty employees browsing with their discounts, and my small morning crew. Still, my body felt heavier with each passing minute.

By mid-shift, it became unbearable. My limbs ached with fatigue, my vision blurred at the edges. I could barely keep my eyes open. I had to go home. I asked the second-shift manager to come in early and, thankfully, they agreed. If my home had been farther than five minutes away, I'm not sure I would have made it. When I arrived, my husband was still there, getting ready for his overnight shift. I asked him to keep our toddler home with me, just in case. I wasn't sure I would be well enough to pick her up from daycare later. "I just need a nap," I reassured him. But that nap turned into something far more terrifying than I ever could have imagined.

When I awoke, it wasn't to the gentle dim light of evening, nor to the sound of my husband returning home. It was morning. Sunlight streamed through the windows, too bright, too sudden. My toddler was asleep on the sofa. And I was on the floor. Confusion hit me first. Why was I in the living room? Why wasn't my daughter in her own bed? I blinked, trying to piece together the fragments of memory, but nothing made sense. The living room was a mess. Blankets were strewn across the floor, and items scattered haphazardly. But I had no recollection of what had happened.

I tried to move. Nothing. Panic flared in my chest. My legs refused to cooperate. I tried again, desperately willing them to work, but they remained lifeless, heavy, unresponsive. My arms fared no better, flopping uselessly when I attempted to lift them. It was a nightmare, except I was fully awake.

Terror crept in like a slow-moving shadow. Had I been drugged? If so by who and when? The thought struck me like a lightning bolt, but no, it wasn't possible. I had never touched drugs, never even taken a sip of alcohol. But then, what was happening to me? Why couldn't I move? The sound of voices jolted me from my spiraling thoughts.

Someone was at the door. Then, the unmistakable sound of a key turning in the lock.

Fear surged through me. My pulse hammered in my ears. I couldn't move, but I could still speak. Summoning every ounce of strength, I screamed a weak, broken sound, but it was all I had. "Get out! I'll call the police!" The door opened. Then, a voice. A familiar one.

Relief washed over me in a tidal wave. It was Channie, my friend, and my co-worker. She had come to check on me after I failed to show up for a manager's meeting that morning. She knew it was unlike me to be absent without notice. When she saw my car still parked outside, an uneasy feeling settled over her. She convinced the apartment maintenance man to unlock the door and perform a wellness check. She had saved me. But as I sat there, paralyzed and terrified, I had no idea what exactly she had saved me from. Or what was still to come.

Channie's face said it all when she saw me. I was a mess of tangled hair, stained with blood, sitting in nothing but an oversized t- shirt. "What happened?" she asked, her voice trembling with concern. I tried to remember, but my mind was fragmented, filled with flashes of jumbled memories that made no sense. Then it hit me. My baby. I frantically touched my stomach to the best of my ability, searching for those reassuring flutters. But there was nothing.

My husband rushed through the door soon after. He had called my workplace when he could not reach me and had been told no one knew where I was. Panicked, he left work early and came straight home. He scooped me up and insisted we go to the hospital. I could not argue. Soon I regained control of my body and limbs again and was able to walk unassisted. Slightly relieved, I was still trying to make sense of what had happened. My memories flickered like a broken film reel, each scene more confusing than the last. Still, I was determined to remember all that I could. But the nightmare was only just beginning.

At the hospital, my mind felt clearer, though I was still wrapped in a thick haze of exhaustion and confusion. But one thought burned through the fog, urgent and undeniable. Something was wrong with my baby. I told the nurses. I told the doctors. I pleaded with them to check me immediately. But they did not take me seriously. They humored me with a blood test, nothing more. And then I saw the doctor pulling my husband aside, whispering something just out of earshot. My heart pounded as I watched my husband's face shift, his expression twisting into something unreadable.

When the doctor returned, he spoke calmly, too calmly, as if he were delivering routine news. "You are not pregnant. You never were." The words slammed into me, stealing the breath from my lungs. "That's not possible," I said, shaking my head. The doctor remained firm, his voice clinical, unmoved. Even if I had miscarried, he explained, the pregnancy test would still show a high hormone count. Mine did not. Therefore, I could not have been pregnant.

Liar. I didn't care what their test claimed. I knew my body. I had been pregnant. I had felt my baby moving inside me just the day before. This was not my first pregnancy. I knew what was real, and I knew what I had lost. I protested. I fought. But the doctor only sighed, rattling off more so-called evidence, listing reasons that refuted my claim. Cold. Detached. Dismissing my words as though they were the ramblings of a woman who had lost touch with reality. And then, the final blow.

Because my new OBGYN had been on vacation, the hospital staff had contacted her office, only to be told that I had not yet been seen by that doctor. There were no records of my pregnancy. No proof. Nothing. That was all they needed. The pitying looks. The hushed tones. The way they suddenly treated me like a fragile, unstable woman teetering on the edge of madness. They even suggested sending me upstairs to the psych ward. I wanted to scream. I wanted to force them to believe me. But what could I do? What words could I say that would make them hear me, make them see me? I wasn't crazy, but they had already decided I was. So I did the only thing I could. I played along. I convinced them to let me go home, promising to follow up with my OBGYN later. I needed to get out of there, away from their disbelieving stares. Away from their suffocating condescension.

Once home, all I wanted was to collapse into bed and let the nightmare fade into oblivion. But then, something caught my eye. The bed sheets were gone. Confused, I asked my husband about it. He didn't know. We searched and found them, bundled up, stained in deep, dark red. My mattress was ruined, soaked through with whatever had happened that night. I stared at the evidence, at the undeniable truth written in blood. And yet, I was too weak, too drained to make sense of it. None of it added up. The hospital had made me question my own sanity, and for one brief, terrifying moment, I wondered. Am I actually crazy? No. No, I wasn't.

I pushed the thought aside. I wasn't the one who was wrong. I wasn't the one who had failed to see the truth. They were. And eventually, I would piece it all together. I just needed sleep. When I woke again, my husband was kneeling beside me, spooning warm soup toward my lips. He had called his mother for advice, and she had insisted I eat something. But I couldn't. I had no appetite. My body was drained, my mind clouded in a thick fog of exhaustion and grief.

I still didn't understand what had happened. I still didn't have answers. What had happened to me? Had something happened to my toddler? Had she been safe through it all? And my baby. What had happened to my baby? The questions gnawed at me, circling my mind even as my body ached for more rest. I let the exhaustion take me again, hoping, praying, that when I woke, things would make sense. And then, in pieces, the memories started to return.

Tiny fragments, like shattered glass catching the light, sharp and incomplete. I remembered waking throughout the night. I remembered my two-year-old, happy and playing, oblivious to my suffering. I remembered being so weak, so impossibly heavy that I could not even form the words to tell her to go to bed. Then—pain.

A terrible, suffocating pressure in my abdomen. A force so strong it brought me to my knees. I remembered crawling, my body barely functioning, making it as far as my bedroom before collapsing. I had been alone. I had been in pain. And something. Something had happened. The memories were scattered, but they were coming back. And I was finally beginning to put the pieces together.

I gripped the phone tightly, my voice unsteady as I explained my theory to the hospital nurse. I had miscarried, and my baby was still in the toilet. Surely, they would help me. Surely, someone would come and take care of what I couldn't bear to face. But the voice on the other end was cold, detached, utterly devoid of empathy. "You'll need to retrieve the remains and bring them to the hospital for verification." The words sliced through me, leaving me breathless. I asked, no, I begged for help. Surely, there was someone, anyone, who could come instead. I wasn't strong enough. I wasn't capable of doing this on my own.

But there was no compassion, no offer of assistance. Just the same cold directive. In that moment, I felt the full, crushing weight of the cruelty life had inflicted upon me. I staggered into the kitchen, grabbed a pot, and returned to the bathroom. My hands trembled violently as I reached into the murky water, my body wracked with silent sobs. Every movement felt impossible, unbearable. And then, there it was. The proof of what I had lost, cradled in my shaking hands. I couldn't look. I placed everything into a black trash bag, my vision blurred with tears. With what little strength I had left, I called the hospital again, clinging to the last shred of hope that someone would finally help me.

The answer was the same. If I wanted help, I had to bring my baby in myself. Exhausted, broken, and barely able to stand, I gathered my toddler and the bag and drove to the hospital. The drive was agonizing, but not as agonizing as the realization that settled over me as I walked toward the entrance. In one hand, I held the warm, tiny fingers of my living child. In the other, I carried the remains of the child I had lost. The cruel irony of it all was suffocating and nothing I would wish on any soul.

Inside, the waiting room was full, an endless sea of people, noise, and indifference. A nurse informed me that the wait would be two to three hours. I blinked at her, struggling to process her words. This can't be real, I thought. I had used every last ounce of my strength to walk through those hospital doors. I had nothing left. I couldn't sit there for hours, holding my grief in a plastic bag, waiting as if this were some ordinary appointment.

I stepped to the intake counter, my movements slow, deliberate. With shaking hands, I placed the bag down and whispered my truth. I voiced what had happened, what I had been told to do. The receptionist hesitated, then nodded, her voice softer than I expected. "I'll take your information. Someone will call you once they've examined it." I turned and walked out, numb. Somehow, I made it home. Somehow, I crawled into bed, my body was too weak to do anything else.

Hours later, the hospital called. This time, the voice on the other end was gentle, filled with an understanding I had desperately needed earlier. She apologized. I had delivered a premature stillborn baby. And then, the truth. The awful, gut-wrenching truth. When my husband and I had come in earlier, the nurse had made a mistake. She had misread my hormone levels, using the wrong measurement. I had been pregnant all along. They were wrong. They had dismissed me, doubted me, and made me question my own reality. Now, they wanted me to come back for an exam. I refused. I no longer trusted them. I wanted nothing to do with that hospital ever again. I would wait and see my OBGYN the next day.

In the days that followed, I tried to heal. I tried to make sense of what had happened, to find my way back to some semblance of normal. But the grief was a living thing, pressing against my chest, always lurking just beneath the surface. I thought I could outrun it. I thought work would be a distraction. Then Dawn walked in. Still out of work, on maternity leave she was glowing, cradling her newborn in her arms. Her baby had been due around the same time as mine. She beamed as she introduced me to her child, her joy radiating through the room. And then, unknowingly, she asked about mine.

The air was sucked from my lungs. I couldn't breathe. I couldn't think. The pain I had buried surged to the surface, threatening to consume me. I shook my head, unable to form words, my body trembling with the force of my sorrow. I needed to get out. I needed to escape before I shattered completely. The last thing I needed was an audience to witness my unraveling. Then, from somewhere close, a quiet voice cut through the suffocating haze of grief.

"Are you okay?" I turned to see William, another coworker. I nodded instinctively. He gave me a knowing smile. "I know you are, but I'll take the next few customers. You can take a break if you want." Such a tiny thing. Such a simple gesture. And yet, it was everything. That moment reminded me that I was not alone. That it was okay not to be okay. Even in the depths of my pain, there were still people who cared.

Losing my baby was the darkest chapter of my life, a wound so deep that I sometimes wondered if I would ever truly heal. To this day, I still do not know the truth of what caused me to miscarry or what happened that night. I may never fully understand. But I made a choice. I chose not to let the little that I do know to be the final words in my story.

Pain touches everyone. My story is painful, yes, but no one has a monopoly on suffering. We all experience loss. We all carry wounds. And because of that, we owe each other kindness, compassion, and understanding. Pain has a way of reshaping us. But it does not have to destroy us. I could have let my grief consume me. I could have let it define me. But instead, I allowed it to transform me.

Every challenge I face now, I remind myself of that night. I remember the storm I survived the strength I discovered within myself. If I could survive that, I can survive anything. From my own experience, I encourage anyone who has experienced deep emotional pain to use it. Use it to grow. Use it to heal. Use it to lift others who may be drowning in the same darkness you once knew.
Pain has a way of reshaping us, but it does not have to harden us. Let it soften you to the struggles of others, deepen your compassion, and ignite a purpose greater than yourself. You are not alone in your suffering, and your story no matter how painful, it can be a beacon of hope for

someone else. Do not let your pain silence you. Let it empower you. Turn it into strength, into wisdom, into something that makes the world a little better because you endured it. Your scars are not just reminders of what you have lost. They are proof of what you have survived. And that survival is a testament to the unbreakable resilience within you.

Self Reflection

In what ways has a painful experience changed how you face other less painful situations?

What helped you endure the moments when you thought you could not continue on?

What evidence do you see in your life that shows that you are more resilient than you once believed?

Is there any meaning or lesson you can draw from that situation not to justify the pain, but to honor what you lived through?

Reflection & Growth

How do you move forward while still honoring the scars of your experience without allowing the pain to become your identity?

What new possibilities for joy, peace, or connection can you imagine for yourself after what you have endured?

From an external perspective, what can you observe about your own strength and worth?

THE FAMILY BOND

Have you ever heard a voice, clear as day, warning you about something? Not a gut feeling or intuition, but an actual voice. If so, you will understand what I am about to share. If not, it might sound strange, even unbelievable. It was an ordinary day. I was at home, alone, sitting at my desk, casually going about my routine. Everything seemed so normal until I heard it. Words as clear as if someone had spoken them right beside me. "Get life insurance on your mother."

I was stunned. It was not a thought I had been having. It was not connected to anything I was doing or thinking at the time. But the message was undeniable, and I could not shake it. Was the voice God, was it me, or my subconscious? In the moment I had no idea. I was certain of what I heard and the subtle intensity behind it. There was no denying what I heard, and I could not let it go.

Buying a life insurance policy for my mother seemed like a logical thing to do. She had been a single parent my entire life and she was nearing retirement. Although the prompt was a bit unusual, I decided to listen to the voice. I began searching online for an insurance policy for my mother. When my husband got home, I told him what I heard. He was puzzled but agreed that I should follow my instincts.

Without hesitation, I found a term policy for my mother and called her for her consent. I did not give her the backstory. Honestly, I was too stressed to explain. There was no need to unnecessarily stress her as well. She was all for getting the policy since she did not have one in place at the time. Getting a life insurance policy was something she had intended to do. She just had not gotten around to doing so at the time. The last thing she wanted was for her children to be responsible for her burial expenses. Once the policy was in place, a wave of relief washed over me. Whether I was acting on some divine insight or just being overly cautious, I knew I had done the right thing.

I figured the coverage was small enough not to stir any family disputes but large enough to cover burial expenses if needed. The only problem was... I was not entirely sure whether the voice had meant my mother or my mother-in-law. Both women had their share of past health issues, but at that moment, both were fine, healthy, even. Life was good. So, using logic, I convinced myself that it must have been about my mother. After all, she was the one living alone, with only me and my two brothers as her immediate family. Plus, the voice specifically mentioned "mother."

I felt confident in my decision. My mother completed her paperwork, and I set the policy on autopay. I prayed that my mother would be healthy and full of life without need of the policy for many years to come. I was hoping for a case of having something just in case and not needing it. For two years I was thankful that my prayers seemed to have been answered. Then, life threw a curveball I was not expecting.

I received a call at work. My mother-in-law had been rushed to the hospital in critical condition. It was completely random. She was fine until the moment she was not. She was diagnosed with a brain aneurysm. The hospital staff did their best, but they could not reverse the damage that had been done. Days later, she passed away. The loss was gut-wrenching for our family. None of us had been prepared, emotionally or otherwise.

As we tried to navigate the grief, the practical reality of planning a funeral only made things worse. The family pressed through the days and funeral arrangements, still in shock and under the cloud of grief. The weight of practical decisions only fueled the tension, intensifying the pain we were already feeling. Emotions boiled over, and old family wounds were reopened. With no true outlet for the pain of grief, the external family tensions somehow rested upon the cost and responsibility of the burial expenses.

Amid the chaos, I found myself reflecting on that voice. It could not have been meant for my mother-in-law, could it? After all, the words had been clear: "your mother." The directive had seemed so straightforward at the time. Yet as I stood in the center of the family turmoil, aching to shoulder the financial burden myself, it hit me. I had overlooked something critical that I was not yet aware of.

I struggled with that moment, replaying it, questioning why I had not acted differently. Why had I been so obtuse in my own thinking? I sought answers from God, praying for clarity. Silence. No response came. After some time, I gave up trying to make sense of it. What was done was done. But the unresolved pain clung to me, and I could not escape the nagging feeling that something important had slipped through my fingers. It was something that might have changed the course of everything.

Sometime later, while reading the Bible, I came across a verse that struck me in a way it never had before. "And the two shall become one flesh." I had heard it countless times, but now, it resonated differently. Just like God is alive, so is His word. In my situation, the Word of God had a new context. It dawned on me that when I married, my husband's family became mine in the same context as my own family. Previously, I used the term in-law as a separate division of family. In the proper context, under the covenant I made with God, my husband's family became mine under God's law. His mother was not just his through birth alone, she was also mine as well in the same context. One may have given birth to me, yet they were equally my mother once I married. All this I thought I understood before but when put to the test those very things had not made it beyond knowledge in my head to true understanding in my heart.

It was a sobering lesson, one that revealed how easily we fall into societal patterns instead of following the deeper principles we believe in. I had also let my own reasoning cloud what I now see was a much broader truth. Had I viewed both mothers equally, I would have approached them with the same care and consideration. I would have had those difficult conversations about life insurance with each of them. I would have planned for both their futures if I did not hold one in higher regard as my mother. Even if I were confused, two life insurance policies would have been a practical choice at the time. Instead, the thought never crossed my mind. Instead, the family's emotions mixed with grief boiled over at the cost of an unexpected funeral for a loved one.

I do not share this story to suggest that every family dynamic is the same or that every decision is straightforward. Relationships are complex, and when two people come together in marriage, the layers of family, tradition, and expectation can make things even more challenging. The biblical principle that the two will become one, goes beyond just the couple. It touches everything around them, especially the blending of two families. And that is not always easy.

When we marry, we do not just unite with our spouse. We take on their joys, their struggles, and yes, their family. This can bring unexpected challenges, different upbringings, varying values, and old family patterns that are not easily broken. It is not as simple as just loving your spouse. It requires loving and embracing the people and dynamics that come with them. The process of becoming one is not always smooth or comfortable. It asks us to stretch beyond ourselves, to make room for more than we ever thought we could.

But when we approach marriage and the families that come with it with the same grace, patience, and selflessness that scripture calls for, we begin to see that this unity is not just about two people. It is about learning to walk in harmony even when the path is uneven, to love each other's family as our own, and to stand together in the face of whatever challenges arise. Taking on the weight of responsibility means more than just meeting our own needs. It involves caring for the well-being of those our spouse holds dear. This does not necessarily mean that extended family members will live together in perfect harmony. Instead, it means that when challenges arise, we respond with the same thoughtfulness, care, and consideration as we would give to our biological loved ones.

This principle of becoming one invites us to go deeper, to put forth the effort to understand and support one another's family dynamics, no matter how complicated they may be. And yes, all families are complicated. In marriage we are to build a sense of unity that extends beyond just the two of us. We are to reach into the relationships that have shaped our spouse's life. In doing so, we create not only a stronger marriage but a foundation of love and unity.

Self Reflection

What does the word family mean to you, beyond blood or legal ties?

What challenges arise in balancing loyalty between biological and inherited family relationships?

When love feels complicated, how do you remind yourself of the humanity behind each relationship?

Growth & Reflection

How can you practice gratitude for the love you've received, even when it shows up in imperfect ways?

What boundaries may you need put in place to protect your well- being while still honoring connection?

What practices do you use to weave all types of family members into the larger fabric of your family ties?

What role do you want to embody in your family, both given and chosen, going forward?

THE CHURCH FOLKS

The second Wednesday of every month was always the best day to be in school. It was a day dedicated to the arts. Professionals from music, art, and athletics fields would rotate through the elementary schools, teaching us in their respective disciplines. Our regular teachers would use the time to plan while we, the students, got a taste of something different. It was a break from the usual routine.

One particular Wednesday, Mr. Hart, our visiting music teacher, rolled his piano cart into the classroom with his usual sense of importance. We were rehearsing a song I did not know, and as my anxiety grew, I found myself absentmindedly chewing on a plastic barrette at the end of my braid. I was an anxious kid by nature, always full of restless energy that needed an outlet. Looking back, I realize this was my way of self-soothing trying to calm the nerves that always seemed to bubble just beneath the surface. But at the time, all I knew was that chewing on that barrette made me feel a little less anxious.

Mr. Hart, however, saw something vastly different. To him, I was not a nervous kid trying to cope. I was distracted, unengaged, and uninterested in his lesson. This was not a graded class, and I had always thought music was supposed to be fun, but Mr. Hart had different expectations. He was looking for full participation, and when I did not give it to him, he decided to make an example out of me.

The music abruptly stopped, and before I knew it, Mr. Hart was standing right in front of me. In a blur of motion, he grabbed me by both wrists, yanked me from my seat, and began to yell. I was so shocked that I could not even process what was happening. Fear surged through me as I dangled helplessly in the air, his grip tight around my wrists. My mind went blank. I did not know what to do, what to say, or even how to feel. All I knew was fear. The terror of the moment was overwhelming.

He berated me loudly in front of the entire class, and then just as quickly as it had begun, he dropped me back into my seat and ordered me to sing. I could not. I could barely breathe, let alone sing. My throat was tight with fear and humiliation, and before I knew it, the tears started.

Crying only made things worse. Mr. Hart looked at me with disgust, dismissing me entirely, telling the class to ignore me as if I was not even there. He resumed his lesson as though nothing had happened.

Thankfully, the day was nearly over. My classmates were eerily silent, perhaps too shocked to say anything. As the final bell rang, I wiped away my tears, dread washing over me as I thought about explaining everything to my mother. I was the kind of kid who never got into trouble, and now I had no idea how to make sense of what had just happened. I did not even understand it myself.

I joined the other children at the crossing guard, waiting to walk across the street where my mother would meet me. But before I could even reach her, some of my classmates rushed ahead and eagerly told her what had happened in music class. I could see her face tighten with anger as she turned to me and asked if it was true. My tears began to fall again. Without another word, she took my hand and said, "Let's go."

We marched back into the school, a trail of second graders following behind like little witnesses to what was about to unfold. My mother was on a mission. Her protective instincts had kicked in, and she was determined to make things right. She stormed into the office, demanding to see the principal and to confront Mr. Hart. She was in full momma bear mode, fierce and unyielding. She wanted justice for what had been done to her child. Her anger was palpable, and no one was going to calm her down until she had her say.

When Mr. Hart was summoned to the office, he did not deny what had happened. He admitted to grabbing me, to yelling, to humiliating me in front of the class. But what was most disturbing was his lack of remorse. He saw nothing wrong with his actions. To him, it was justified. The principal, on the other hand, was mortified. She apologized profusely, trying to soothe my mother's outrage. My mother demanded that Mr. Hart stay far away from me from that point forward, believing he was a threat.

In response, the principal came up with a plan. From then on, I would sit in the office during music class each month, ensuring I would not have to interact with Mr. Hart again. But as a child, I could not help but feel like I was the one being punished. I had not done anything wrong, yet I was the one who had to sit out of class, isolated from my peers. It felt unfair, like I was being made to carry the burden of an adult's wrongdoing.

A few weeks later, I was sitting in my grandmother's living room on a quiet Sunday morning. The TV was on, and to my utter disbelief, there was Mr. Hart, singing and praising the Lord on a public access channel. He was leading worship, smiling and joyful, proclaiming his love for God. I could not believe my eyes. How could someone who had treated me so cruelly, with such anger and harshness, now stand there in front of a congregation, calling himself a Christian? How could he lead others in praise and worship, yet act with such disregard for a child's feelings?

In that moment, something deep within me shifted, and my perspective darkened. The hypocrisy I witnessed in Mr. Hart did not just tarnish my view of him, it cast a shadow over my view of all Christians. If someone like Mr. Hart could stand as a representative of the church, then perhaps the entire institution was a facade. Maybe the faith I had been taught to cherish was nothing more than a mask, a convenient disguise for people hiding their true selves.

For years, that single experience left a bitter taste in my mouth. It caused me to distrust people who claimed to be Christians, all because of one man's actions. I could not bring myself to trust believers the way I was taught to trust God. In my mind, all believers were cut from the same cloth. If Mr. Hart could live such a double life, fooling others with his polished performance, who could I trust?

As a child, I had seen the church as sacred ground, a place where people truly revered and feared God. I believed it was a space where holiness reigned, and hypocrisy would be met with swift judgment. But what I saw that day shattered those beliefs. Instead of being confronted, Mr. Hart was celebrated. The congregation applauded the man they thought they knew, blind to the mask he wore. The dissonance was staggering, and I was left questioning everything I once held dear.

As I matured in life, I found that scenario repeated itself in different forms, through different people. I began to understand the deeper significance and the moral of my experiences. As Christians, we represent Christ in every aspect of our lives, not just in church or when we are around other believers, but in our daily interactions. The way we treat others, especially the vulnerable, is one of the largest representations.

Our behavior speaks volumes, often louder than our words. When our actions do not align with the teachings of God, people notice. It is not just the obvious behaviors that matter, but the subtle ones too. We cannot claim to be followers of Christ, walking in His light, yet treat others with cruelty, anger, or indifference. What we project on the outside reflects the Spirit of God within us. Our words and actions have power, they can either inspire belief or destroy it. When they do not align with the love of God, we risk turning people away from the Kingdom, sometimes without even realizing it.

Let my story serve as a reminder, we carry the responsibility of reflecting Christ in all we do. Our faith is not just a set of beliefs, it is a way of life that others see and feel. We never know who is watching or how our behavior might influence someone's journey of faith. In every interaction, we have the opportunity to reflect Christ's love, grace, and compassion, or to do the opposite. And that choice is one we carry with us every day.

Self Reflection

Do you sometimes place people of religious faith on a pedestal that doesn't leave room for their humanity?

How do you discern between healthy imperfection and harmful hypocrisy as you continue life as a representation of your faith?

Do you extend the same compassion to others in their struggles that you hope they would extend to you?

How can you hold yourself accountable for aligning your actions with your beliefs, while still allowing grace for your own humanity?

Growth & Reflection

What would a realistic, compassionate expectation of church community look like?

What can you do to focus on living your own faith with integrity, rather than measuring others against ideals?

Have you ever confused outward displays of faith with true inner character? What does true inner character look like?

Where do you see genuine examples of lived-out faith, and how can you let those inspire you?

THE REPRESENTATYON

There is something uniquely comforting about being home alone after a long day. The relief, contentment, and excitement of having absolutely nothing to do is a feeling that is hard to beat. That was exactly how I felt one evening, determined to savor peace and quiet. Then, the doorbell rang. I was not expecting anyone, but curiosity got the better of me, so I answered. Standing before me was a petite, middle-aged woman. She could likely see from my expression that I was not thrilled by her unannounced visit. Sensing my hesitation, she quickly introduced herself as Emily, one of my neighbors.

Her friendliness softened my guard a bit, and I invited her in to hear about the "important neighborhood matter" she had come to discuss. Once inside, Emily shared her story. She lived in our neighborhood on a lot that bordered a protected area. A few weeks earlier, she had removed several trees without the permission of the community we lived in. This act had harmed the protected area, and she now faced a lawsuit from the developer demanding a substantial amount in damages. Emily, desperate and distraught, was collecting signatures from neighbors to petition against the claim, hoping that enough support might lessen her legal woes. She admitted it was a long shot, but with four young children and such a staggering lawsuit hanging over her family, she had to try.

    As she spoke, something in my gut told me not to get involved. Yet, despite this intuition, I hesitated. My eyes caught sight of the shiny gold crucifix hanging around Emily's neck, and that small, symbolic detail swayed me. I rationalized that as fellow Christians, we should help each other. What would Jesus do, right? Wrong. A familiar religious symbol should have meant nothing but at that moment it did. What Jesus may have actually done, would have been to size up that person's heart and motive before doing anything. Against my better judgment, I took the pen she offered and signed the petition. The instant regret was palpable.

    Emily's face lit up in gratitude, and she confessed that I was one of the few neighbors willing to go against the powerful developer. Everyone else was too intimidated. As she left, a wave of foolishness washed over me. I could not shake the feeling that I had been too quick to jump into a fight that I knew nothing about. Why did I let an ornate object, a crucifix, convince me to ignore my instincts? I had just made a decision that went against my instinct, and for what?

Reflecting on the evening, I realized the mistakes I had made. First, I did not need to answer the door in the first place. It was my home, my peaceful evening, and I had no obligation to entertain uninvited visitors. Second, I ignored the clear warning signs my gut was giving me. Finally, I broke my personal rule. Never sign anything under pressure. I normally waited a minimum of 24 hours before giving my signature to anything. Commitment to something, especially when it involves complicated matters, should be carefully weighed. Yet here I was, letting a familiar religious symbol cloud my judgment.

The next day, determined to right my wrong, I paid Emily a visit. I explained that I had second thoughts about signing her petition and that I did not fully understand the complexity of her situation. To my relief, Emily was gracious. She understood my hesitation and agreed to remove my name from the petition. As I waited for her to retrieve the document, I noticed the expensive artwork adorning her walls and the grand piano in her living room. It hit me: Emily and I were not cut from the same circumstances. She was wealthy and had access to resources for her problems that I did not have. I was not in a position to make enemies from being entangled in a lawsuit over tree removal that pitted the rich and the wealthy against one another when I did not fit either category.

Emily returned with the petition and, true to her word, scratched through my name. She was considerate to use white out to further remove my name from the document. She revealed that the only other signature on the petition was her husband's. In that moment, I felt reassured. I was making the right decision. This was not my battle to fight. I was so outside of my element that I could not help Emily if I wanted to.

In the months that followed, Emily and the developer went back and forth over their legal issues and reached and agreement. Emily moved to California after inheriting a sizable estate, and the developer went on to become one of the largest in our state. The whole situation worked out as I had expected. The rich got richer, and I returned to my quiet, content life.

Although I never really got to know Emily on a deeper personal level, I don't think she was being deceptive. She was just trying to win a tough situation with whatever support she could find locally. Getting people to sign something was probably a lot cheaper and easier for her than paying a settlement to the developer.

Honestly, I think she reacted the way most people would in her shoes. It was calculated, maybe, but not unreasonable. As for the crucifix necklace she wore, I'll never know if it was a deliberate choice to gain sympathy or just something she always wore. Either way, I hope she learned something from the experience. I know I did. No matter how convincing or passionate someone may seem, it is essential to first seek God's counsel. Then trust your intuition, and let wisdom guide your steps. People can be persuasive, their causes compelling, but without discernment, it is all too easy to get swept up in something that was never meant for you.

Just like her fight against the developer, everything about Emily's cause looked straightforward at first. It had all the elements of urgency, a relatable problem, and a genuine call for support. She had a cause, and she was rallying for people to stand with her. It was tempting to join in. I instinctively knew it was not my fight, but I allowed the possibility of us having a shared faith sway me. Honestly, I should have looked for a larger motive before jumping into the situation. It could have easily been a ploy to deceive me for my support.

But then something else important hit me. Not every battle is mine to fight. If I had jumped in, I might have ended up tangled in a conflict that didn't truly involve me, facing off against people who were never meant to be my enemies. Sometimes the wisest thing you can do is recognize when a fight, no matter how just it seems, simply isn't yours. It is easy to get drawn into a struggle when someone approaches you with an issue that feels personal and relatable. But wisdom whispers louder than any persuasively spoken word if we take the time to listen. Wisdom will tell you, there are fights for which we are not equipped for, struggles that require tools and armor we have not yet forged. Entering into such fights prematurely can leave you wounded and stranded, grappling with consequences that were not yours to bear.

With the lesson firmly absorbed, I returned to savoring my peaceful evenings. From now on, I answer the door with sharper discernment, unclouded by symbols or ideals that might compromise good judgment. True understanding lies in embracing wisdom and trusting the quiet guidance of intuition, principles I intend to carry forward.

Self Reflection

Do you give more grace to someone from your faith community than to someone outside of it?

How might your assumptions about shared faith cause you to dismiss, undervalue, or misjudge others?

Have you ever made someone feel excluded because they didn't share your faith?

How does relying on shared faith as a "shortcut" for trust prevent you from discerning a person's true character?

Growth & Reflection

How can you remind yourself that faith is lived out in action, not only in labels or affiliation?

In what ways might recognizing bias help you deepen your compassion for people of all backgrounds?

Is there someone outside your faith that has modeled love, wisdom, or integrity in ways that surprised or challenged you?

If you released your bias, how might your relationships, worldview, or faith itself expand?

How can you practice seeing people first as human beings, with shared dignity, before filtering them through faith identity?

THE DISMAY

If the dictionary had pictures, mine would be right next to the word. My mother, always one to speak her mind without hesitation or filter, had left me utterly stunned. I had just hung up the phone after sharing what was, to me, the biggest news of my life. It was news that filled my heart with a heady mix of nerves and excitement. I was getting married. I do not know exactly what I expected her to say. Congratulations, or perhaps a little excitement to match my own, but what I received was something else entirely.

After I told her that my boyfriend had proposed, there was an extended silence on her end of the line. Not the kind of silence that feels like processing, but the sort that feels deliberate. When she finally spoke, her words were careful, measured, and entirely unlike the fiery directness that usually defined her. She started by reminding me of a truth I already knew. She had made the conscious decision never to marry. My mother had always been a fiercely independent woman, wearing her single status as both a badge of honor and a shield against vulnerability.

"This is your choice," she said firmly. "Only yours to make." She went on to admit that she did not have much to offer in the way of wisdom about marriage. For a woman who always seemed to have something to say about everything, this admission alone was a revelation. Then, as though she had been saving it for just this moment, her tone shifted. She softened, her voice dropping lower, almost conspiratorial, as if she were about to impart some profound truth. Leaning into the receiver, I braced myself for the rare moment when my mother, so often pragmatic and unsentimental, might reveal something deeply personal. Perhaps she would share a story about her own life, something raw and vulnerable that might bridge the gap between her experience and my own. And then, with all the weight of wisdom passed down through the ages, she said, "Never buy a man a pair of shoes, or he'll walk out of your life."

That was it. That was her big advice. I remember sitting there, blinking at the receiver, utterly baffled. My initial response was to laugh, not because it was funny, but because it felt so absurd. It was the kind of advice that might be scribbled inside of a fortune cookie or delivered as the punchline of a joke. Shoes? Really? That is what my mother had for me at this momentous crossroads in my life?

The conversation ended shortly after, leaving me both amused and bewildered. I spent days trying to decipher her words, searching for some hidden layer of wisdom. Was it symbolic? Was it rooted in some cultural or personal experience I did not understand? But no matter how I twisted and turned it in my mind, it remained exactly what it seemed, a strange and nonsensical old wives' tale. If this was the great gem of relationship wisdom passed down through the women in my family, I, we were all doomed. At eighteen years old, standing at the precipice of marriage, shoes felt like the least of my concerns.

Eventually, I let it go, burying the memory alongside the countless other odd quirks that made up my mother's personality. Years passed, and I did not think about her words again until I became a mother myself. Parenthood has a funny way of forcing you to reexamine your past, of holding up a mirror to your own upbringing and asking, what will you keep? What will you leave behind?

It was only then, standing in the role my mother had once held, that her words began to take on new meaning. I realized that the advice was not about shoes, or even about men, at all. It was about offering the best she could in that moment. My mother, for all her independence and strength, did not have a wealth of wisdom to share about relationships. She had not walked the road I was preparing to embark on. But she loved me, and she wanted to give me something. Like the widow in the Bible who gave two small coins because it was all she had, my mother offered me the only advice she could pull from her limited vault of experience.

Looking back, her words were less about practicality and more about intention. They were a gesture of love, however imperfect. She gave what she had, hoping it might mean something to me, and in doing so, she passed down something deeper than I initially realized. It was a reminder that love does not always come wrapped in neat, tidy packages. Sometimes, it is messy, awkward, and even strange, but it is love all the same.

Becoming a mother brought other realizations, too. That phone call was not just a snapshot of my mother's eccentricity. It was a reflection of the gaps in our family's ability to communicate. We had spoken about so many things over the year, politics, work, societal constructs, but we had rarely, if ever, touched the truly vulnerable parts of our hearts. Like many families, we had mastered the art of surface level conversations while leaving the deeper waters unexplored.

I decided then and there that I wanted something different for my children. When it came to the tough conversations, I would not just approach them cautiously. I was determined to embrace them fully. I would build a relationship with my children that prioritized truth, openness, and emotional honesty. My mother's gift to me was her best effort. My gift to my children would be building upon that foundation to create something stronger.

And in that way, my mother gave me more than just an old wives' tale about shoes. She gave me the motivation to do better, to break the cycle of silence, and to pass down a legacy that truly matters. Looking back, her advice may not have been what I wanted, but it was exactly what I needed. It was a reminder that love, in all its imperfect forms, is always worth passing on.

Self Reflection

Have you experienced a situation when the advice didn't meet your needs or situation? How did you feel in the moment?

What intention might the other person have had in offering their advice, even if it missed the mark?

What beauty or humanity can you notice in the act of someone wanting to be there for you, even imperfectly?

Could there be a fragment of truth, wisdom, or perspective in the advice, even if most of it doesn't apply?

Growth & Reflection

How can you use your prior experience to become more thoughtful when you give advice to others?

What can you learn about yourself by noticing what advice to reject and what resonates with you?

THE FIGHT OR FLIGHT

Seeing the flashing blue lights in my rearview mirror was the last thing I expected that night. Barely a year had passed since I got my driver's license, and it had only been two weeks since I got my car. Both were milestones I was proud of. Getting pulled over by the police though, was not part of the plan. A rush of emotions surged through me as I carefully eased over to the side of the road. Panic twisted in my stomach, but it was oddly paired with a bizarre sense of calm. My eyes darted to the speedometer. I was driving well below the legal limit. I had not broken any rules, or at least none that I was aware of. Surely, there was no reason to worry. Right?

Earlier that day, my mood had been joyful. I had just returned to Virginia after a memorable trip to Georgia, where I attended my boyfriend's Army Airborne graduation. It had been a special occasion, one that marked his success after weeks of grueling physical and mental training. The journey to Georgia, however, was a story of its own.

Unintentionally, I had timed my drive south on course with Hurricane Opal's destructive path up the East Coast. The relentless rain battered my windshield, and the howling winds jostled my car as I tried to maintain control. My car hydroplaned once already and feared the results of a second. At some point, I decided it was safer to pull into a restaurant parking lot and wait for the worst of the storm to pass. Hours later, when the wind finally calmed, I resumed my journey, shaken but determined to make it to the base on time. Despite the stress of the drive, my youthful optimism helped me shake off the experience.

The graduation ceremony was a proud and emotional moment. My boyfriend had the choice of receiving his wings from an instructor or from one of his guests. To my surprise and delight, he chose me. Standing there, carefully pinning his wings onto his uniform, I felt an immense sense of pride. Watching the other graduates, I was glad he had opted out of the alternative tradition known as "blood wings." This gruesome ritual involved instructors driving the sharp pins of the badge directly into the graduates' chests, leaving puncture wounds that bled, thus creating "blood wings." I silently thanked him for sparing us both the discomfort of that scene.

After a weekend of celebration, I said my goodbyes and prepared for the long drive back to Virginia. Before leaving, I noticed something unsettling. My temporary license plate was missing. The flimsy piece of card stock must have been destroyed by the hurricane's fierce winds and pounding rain. Thankfully, Virginia required plates on both the front and rear of the vehicle. I came up with a quick fix. I removed the front plate and placed it against the brake light inside the back window, making sure it was visible. Having only one remaining tag, I did not want to risk losing it too. Satisfied with my solution, I began the journey home.

When I finally arrived, I parked my car and felt a wave of relief. The storm, the long hours on the road, and the weekend's excitement were now behind me. The next morning, I busied myself with chores around the house and realized I needed groceries. I jotted down a quick shopping list, grabbed my car keys, and headed out. Everything seemed perfectly ordinary, until I saw those blue lights flashing in my mirror.

I pulled over, expecting a straightforward interaction. I expected the officer to ask for my license and registration. I would comply and soon be on my way. Little did I know this stop was far from routine. The officer, a woman with a commanding and aggressive tone, barked orders as she approached my car with her gun drawn. "Put your hands on the steering wheel! Don't move!" Her voice was sharp and unrelenting. Startled, I obeyed immediately, my palms gripping the wheel tightly. Despite my effort to appear calm and cooperative, I could feel the weight of suspicion in her gaze.

Unsure of what I had done wrong, I tried to ask for clarification. Instead of answering, she fired off questions of her own. "Whose car is this? Where did you get it?" "It's my car," I replied, my voice steady despite my confusion. "I bought it two weeks ago." She was not satisfied. "Where's your license plate?" "It's in the back window," I explained, hoping to reassure her. But my response only seemed to aggravate her further. She side stepped slightly to the rear of the car to check, and when she returned, her demeanor shifted from stern to outright hostile. Her next words were chilling. "You know, it would've been your fault if I'd blown your head off for thinking this car was stolen!"

The shock of her statement hit me like a physical blow. "Blown my head off?" The words echoed in my mind, incomprehensible and terrifying. My pulse quickened as I tried to process what I was hearing. It was a callous and casual way to describe the potential ending of my life. The realization struck me that based on her logic, my life was worth ending over an automobile. It was illogical to think her judgement as a police officer was that my human life was fair trade for a man-made possession. I realized I was momentarily in the care, custody, and control of an irrational person. This was an occasion where my intentionality was vital.

Desperately trying to keep the situation from escalating further, I asked if I could retrieve my license and registration. My movements were slow and deliberate as I moved only my eyes and mouth as I waited for her permission. Despite this being my first encounter with law enforcement, I was certain it was not supposed to unfold like this.

With her weapon holstered, and her hand resting on top of it, I could not help but glance at it, my heart pounding in my chest. I resolved to remain perfectly still, determined not to give her anything to react to. When she finally instructed me to hand over my documents, I did so with painstaking care, always keeping my other hand visible on the steering wheel. Fortunately, I had taken both my license and registration out when I pulled over and placed them in the passenger seat.

As she returned to her patrol car to run my information, I sat frozen, both hands back to gripping the steering wheel. Alone with my thoughts, I replayed the encounter in my mind, grappling with the fear and disbelief that had settled over me. How had a routine traffic stop turned into a moment where my life felt so precariously fragile? Why did my attempts to comply, to remain calm, and to exude respect seem utterly invisible to her? I had no answers, only a sinking feeling that this moment would stay with me forever.

Beneath the surface, a primal instinct to protect myself flared up. It was an undeniable, very human reaction, a deep, internal urge to defend my life and my dignity. But that instinct was at odds with the reality of the situation. This was no time for fight or flight. The literal law and the dynamic of the moment demanded compliance, and compliance alone. Even though I understood this intellectually, my survival instincts screamed in defiance, urging me to act. I forced myself to remain still, my mind racing through potential responses and their consequences. One wrong move, one ill-timed word, could escalate an already precarious situation.

I took a deep breath and began to strategize. This was not just about who was right or wrong. It was about leaving this encounter intact, physically, emotionally, and legally. Reacting, even verbally, would do me no good here. My best chance at a favorable outcome was to be the level-headed person in the situation. Perhaps this officer was having a bad day. Perhaps she was new to the force, unsure of herself and compensating with aggression. Or perhaps she felt she had something to

prove to herself, her peers, or the world. The reasons for her behavior did not really matter to me in that moment. What mattered was walking away from the interaction alive, unharmed, and without legal trouble.

As I sat there gripping the steering wheel, I reminded myself of something vital. I was an eighteen-year-old black young woman, living in a city that was currently vying for one of the top three spot on the US Murder Capital rankings. In the mind of the police officer, I was already guilty of something, or a statistic waiting to be proven guilty. I could not afford to give her anything to support her assumptions. Recalling that her logic was that a stolen car would equate to her "blowing off my head" convinced me of a truth. This officer was a time bomb, and I needed to diffuse the situation for my benefit.

When she finally returned to my car, her demeanor remained sharp and critical. She handed me a warning, her voice dripping with disdain as she delivered more scolding remarks. "It's not my job to look in the rear window of your car," she snapped. "It's my job to check the license plate holder." Her logic was flawed and her tone antagonistic, but I bit my tongue. I wanted to counter her statement, to point out the absurdity of her reasoning. After all, I had done everything within my power to make my temporary tag visible given the circumstances. But I stopped myself. This was not the time or place to argue. I recognized that pushing back, no matter how justified I felt, would only prolong the encounter, and possibly provoke a worse outcome.

Instead, I focused on what truly mattered to me at that moment, leaving this encounter unscathed and free. Winning the argument was not worth the risk of escalating tensions. As she continued to speak, I forced myself to stay calm, nodding politely and offering no resistance. Whatever personal issues or professional insecurities fueling her behavior, none of it was my burden to bear.

The experience left me shaken, but it also taught me a powerful lesson about discernment and self-control. There are moments in life when standing your ground is necessary, even noble. But there are also moments when survival, safety, and self-preservation take precedence over being "right." This was one of those moments. I chose to protect what mattered most: my well-being, my peace, and my future.

As I drove away, the tension in my body slowly began to release. I replayed the encounter in my mind, reflecting on the choices I had made. While part of me wanted to cling to indignation and frustration, I knew I had done the right thing. Sometimes, strength is not about fighting; it is about knowing when to let go, when to prioritize the bigger picture over the heat of the moment. And that day, the bigger picture was clear. My life and freedom were far too valuable to risk over an argument, no matter how justified and right I might have felt.

Self Reflection

How do you typically respond to situations of bias and unfairness? Is fueled with anger, frustration, withdrawal, acceptance, etc.?

Can you identify moments where you responded calmly despite feeling wronged? What helped you do that?

What practices or mindsets help you regain composure when you feel injustice or inequity?

Growth & Reflection

Are there lessons hidden in unfair situations that you might miss if you react impulsively?

How can accepting what you cannot change coexist with a personal commitment to advocating for what is right?

How can recognizing the complexity of life's unfairness deepen your patience, compassion, and desire for doing what is right?

How can you move on from situations of unfairness without resentment and bitterness towards the perpetrators?

THE OBSERVANT

I walked down the street, feeling the cool breeze against my skin as I casually took in my surroundings. Up ahead, I noticed a guy. There was something about him that caught my attention, a certain energy that drew my eyes to him. As I got closer, our eyes met, and for a moment, time seemed to stretch. There was that familiar moment of acknowledgment between two strangers who suddenly are not so strange. "What's up?" he said with a nod, his voice smooth and confident. I offered a simple "Hey," keeping it casual, but internally, I was already bracing myself. I could tell from the look in his eyes what was coming next. Sure enough, right on cue, he asked for my name and number.

He was cute, no denying that. He had that easy charm, the kind that made me feel comfortable despite only just meeting him. He seemed nice enough, too. So, why not? I gave him my number and continued on my way, heading toward my original destination. I was not stressed about it. If he called, he called. If he did not, no big deal. Lately, life had been like that. Like kind of game where people exchanged numbers like trading cards, waiting to see if there was a real connection behind the initial spark.

Later that evening, as I was winding down, my phone rang. Glancing at the screen, I recognized the number. It was him, the guy I had met earlier that day. My curiosity piqued, I answered. "Hey, it's me, D Jay," he said, reminding me of our brief encounter that morning. We started talking, and what began as light conversation quickly evolved into something deeper. We did not just skim the surface of polite introductions. We dove into our lives, family, friends, our dreams, and even the trivial things that irritated us. The conversation flowed easily, and I found myself laughing more than I had in a while. Before I knew it, the clock read 1 a.m. It had felt like only moments had passed.

That phone call was not just a one-time thing. It became our routine. Night after night, D Jay and I would talk for hours, the conversations becoming more personal, more revealing. Eventually, we decided to meet up in person again, planning for the following weekend. I was not sure where things were headed with him. I could not deny there was something there, some potential, some spark that made me want to see where this might lead.

As we spent more time talking, I started to piece together more of who D Jay was. I learned that he did not live in my neighborhood at all. He had just been visiting that day when we met. He lived on the opposite side of the city with his aunt and uncle, who had raised him. The more I learned, the more questions I had. But I did not pry too much. I figured there would be time for that later. He spoke highly of his aunt and uncle, which reassured me. It was clear he had a strong, supportive relationship with them, and that was enough for me at the moment. I did not feel the need to press for every detail of his life just yet.

Still, there was one thing I did not get to ask. A question that kept nagging at the back of my mind like a reminder when I was conversing with him. Who had D Jay been visiting that day we met? It seemed like such an obvious thing to ask, but in the flurry of conversation, I had completely forgotten to bring it up. And now, it felt too late to casually slip it in. We had both made it clear that we were single, but I could not help but wonder if he had been seeing someone else when we first crossed paths. I was not interested in getting caught up in any drama, and I definitely was not going to compete with another young woman for his attention. If it ever came to that, I would bow out without hesitation. Still, the curiosity ate at me, and I made a mental note to ask him next time we spoke.

Normally, I would have told my best friend everything about D Jay. She and I shared everything, but for some reason, I kept him to myself. It was not that I was trying to hide anything. It just did not feel like the right time to bring him up. Our budding relationship was too new, too uncertain. If something real developed, then there would be plenty to talk about. For now, it was just me and D Jay, sharing our nights over the phone, while my days were spent working my job and hanging out with my best friend.

One afternoon, while my friend and I were sitting on her front porch, enjoying the fresh air, and chatting about nothing important, I noticed something strange. An odd brown, Scooby Doo-looking van rolled down the street and parked across the way. It was not anything special, just an old, beat-up van that might not have caught anyone else's attention. But something about it felt off to me. My friend kept talking, completely oblivious, but I could not take my eyes off the van.

After a moment, I realized why it seemed so familiar. D Jay was inside. He sat behind the wheel, his window rolled down as music drifted out. My first instinct was to wave, maybe even walk over to say hello, but something in my gut stopped me. I did not know what it was, just a feeling that something was not right. So, I stayed put, watching him from a distance. He seemed to be looking for someone, glancing around as if he expected to spot someone any second. It struck me as odd, and the longer I watched, the more uneasy I felt. After about twenty minutes, D Jay suddenly started the van and drove off without a word.

I sat there, feeling unsettled. Why hadn't D Jay mentioned that he would be in my neighborhood? Why hadn't he told me he drove such an odd-looking van? Questions flooded my mind, adding to the list of things I wanted to ask him. But when the time for our usual phone call came that night, my phone remained silent. I tried calling him, but there was no answer. Still, I did not panic. Maybe something had come up. He would call back, right? Only, he did not. Not that night, not the next. Days passed in silence, and just like that, D Jay disappeared as suddenly as he had appeared.

I tried calling him a few more times, but eventually, I had to accept that our brief connection had ended. It was not like me to chase after someone, and even if it had been,

I would not have known where to start. Fortunately, I had not invested enough in D Jay to be heartbroken. Life moved on, and D Jay became a distant memory, just another fleeting moment in the landscape of life.

Months passed, and I had nearly forgotten about D Jay when a random conversation jolted me back to that time. I was out, minding my own business, when I overheard two women talking nearby. Their conversation did not interest me at first, but then one of them mentioned a name that I had not heard in a while. Clearly I heard, Dominico, D Jay's real name. When preparing me to potentially meet his family, D Jay disclosed to me his birth name which was uncommon for our city. Since his family and close friends referred to him as Dominico, he wanted to prepare me. My heart skipped a beat, and I leaned in just a little, listening more intently to the women talking. They were talking about him and a major drug bust he had been caught in. He was facing life in prison for the large quantity of drugs he was caught trafficking.

I could not believe what I was hearing. D Jay? The same guy who had charmed me with his easygoing conversation and laughter. That guy was too polite and charming to be a major drug dealer. At least that's what I thought. According to these women, the bust had happened shortly after I saw him in that van. The feds had been monitoring him for some time. During a drug sting operation, they caught him in possession of a very large quantity of drugs.

Everything fell into place at that moment. Him not living in the neighborhood but frequently visiting nameless people. Him disappearing into thin air- it all made sense now. I could not believe it. I realized how close I had come to a dangerous situation without even knowing it. My mind raced with the possibilities. What if I had walked over to that van? What if I had waived him down or spoken to him that day? I could have easily been caught up in something far bigger than myself. Thank God I had stayed back and watched in silence.

When I got home that evening, I rifled through old newspapers, determined to confirm what I had overheard. And there it was, D Jay's full name, right there in black and white, linked to a major drug bust. The realization hit me hard. I had narrowly avoided a world of trouble without even knowing it. I could have been mistaken as an accomplice, drug associate, or caught in whatever net that was cast by the authorities in the bust.

From that moment on, D Jay became a lesson I would not forget. People could tell you whatever they wanted, weave stories with their words, but their actions would always reveal the truth. Words can be manipulated, but actions? They never lied. As the weight of everything settled in, I realized just how much I had been spared by holding back that day, by trusting my instincts rather than rushing forward.

It dawned on me that in a world where words can be dressed up to mask intentions, it is our actions, those unguarded, unfiltered moments, that reveal the truth of who we are. D Jay had been charming, smooth, and easy to talk to. His words painted a picture of a young man who was funny, kind, and full of potential. But when I peeled back the layers, when I stopped letting his words alone carry the weight of who he was, it became clear that something did not add up. His actions,
though subtle, were what ultimately held the truth.

I realized then the importance of being slow to speak and cautious to react, especially when something inside you, the quiet voice of instinct, tells you to wait. In that pause, in that space where I chose not to rush forward, I gained clarity. It was not about being cynical or mistrusting. It was about self-preservation and wisdom, about giving space and time to see people for who they truly are rather than who they claim to be. D Jay taught me a lesson without even knowing it. Sometimes, silence is your strongest ally. It allows you to observe, to watch, and to discern what lies beneath the surface.

There is a power in patience, in resisting the urge to be swept up in the immediacy of someone else's story. Words can build fantasies, offer promises, and create illusions. Actions, those steady consistent behaviors, are what reveal the truth of a person's character. Looking back, I realized how many times I had been quick to trust words over actions, how often I had allowed the stories told to me to overshadow what was right in front of my eyes.

I began to understand that to truly know someone, you must let time reveal who they are. You cannot rush into assumptions or let your emotions cloud your judgment. The truth, I have learned, unfolds gradually, in the small, often unnoticed actions that people take when they think no one is watching. I had almost missed that with D Jay. I had been so caught up in the thrill of new conversations, the excitement of potential, that I nearly overlooked the inconsistencies in his behavior.

But from then on, I promised myself I would not let that happen again. I would be slower to react, slower to speak. I would let people show me who they were through their actions, through how they moved in the world, rather than just through their words. I would give myself the space to observe, to listen not just with my ears but with my intuition, to allow people's behaviors to speak for them in ways that words never could.

It was a quiet but profound shift in my understanding of relationships and life in general. Not everything needs an immediate response or explanation. Sometimes, the most powerful thing you can do is to step back and let time do the talking. Because in that space, in that stillness, the truth has room to reveal itself. And once it does, there is no mistaking it.

Self Reflection

Have you ever had quick reactions that led to outcomes you later regretted?

How can observing a situation fully before responding change your perspective or understanding?

What differences can you notice between acting out of emotion versus acting from awareness?

How can observing first strengthen your communication, decision- making, or relationships?

Growth & Reflection

When has patience and quiet observation revealed solutions or insights you would have otherwise missed?

How can embracing stillness cultivate wisdom, empathy, or emotional balance in your life?

What small daily practices can help you strengthen the habit of observing before acting?

THE UNSEEN DESPAIR

The moment I realized what had happened, a cold wave of dread washed over me. I ran the numbers again, hoping that I had made a mistake, but the math did not lie. There was no escape from it. This month was going to be a minefield, and we were dangerously close to the edge. Our budget had always been tight, a delicate balance that required precision and discipline to keep from tipping over. But this time, it was more than just tight. It was on the verge of collapsing.

My husband's military paycheck had come up short due to an administrative error at work. They assured us it would be corrected, and the missing pay would be added to his next check. But that was little comfort in the moment because our bills would not be waiting patiently for the correction. The deadlines for the electric bill, rent, and groceries were not moving, and with less money in hand, we were facing a financial avalanche that was about to bury us if we did not act quickly.

It hit hard because we did not have the safety net, we had been working so hard to build. We knew the importance of savings and had made it a priority. But life, relentless and unpredictable, had its own way of tearing through our plans. Every time we started to make progress, an unexpected car repair or a sudden household emergency would swoop in, devouring every dollar we had managed to tuck away. And just like that, our savings evaporated. Neither of us had come from families with strong financial foundations. Wealth? Financial literacy? Those were not things we grew up with. We were learning as we went along, but this time, the lesson came with a sense of urgency that was almost suffocating.

So, we did what we could. We thinned out my husband's paycheck, stretching it as far as possible to cover the most critical bills. The essentials were gas, utilities, and rent for the roof over our heads. But even after that, there was barely anything left for groceries. We trimmed that budget down to the bone, preparing to make do with whatever food we had in the cabinets and fridge, hoping it would last until the next paycheck rolled in. It felt like we were navigating a financial tightrope. One wrong step could send everything crashing down. We were trying to remain calm, trying to keep our heads above water, but deep down, we knew the next few weeks would be anything but easy.

The first week was tough, but we managed to make it through. We had crafted a plan, and though it was not perfect, it was enough to get us by for a little while. We stretched what little we had with a series of pasta dishes, creatively reusing leftovers to make them last for several nights. Our meals were repetitive, sure, but they kept us fed. At that point, we were cautiously optimistic.

But as the second week crept up on us, that optimism began to erode. Each day seemed to close in on us a little tighter, and payday still felt far away. We watched with a sense of growing dread as our refrigerator and cabinet shelves became more and more barren. It was like watching water evaporate in the desert, slowly at first, and then all at once. The meals that had sustained us the week before seemed like a distant memory. Sandwiches became our go-to solution, and we tried every variation we could think of. Ham and cheese, grilled cheese, peanut butter and jelly, even toast and jelly when the options grew thinner. But soon, the bread ran out too. With nothing left, we turned to cereal and milk, clinging to that final stretch of hope. But then, inevitably, the milk ran out too. That is when it hit us. We were officially out of food, out of money, and out of options.

It was a sinking feeling that coincided with the worst possible timing, the day before payday. We had nothing left to bridge the gap, and no more tricks up our sleeves. What made it all the more unbearable was that no one knew the situation we were in. From the outside, everything seemed normal. We had a roof over our heads, we had good jobs, we were not destitute. Yet here we were, out of food with another day to go before we could even think about buying more. It was a situation I never thought possible for us. Before, I had always assumed that not having enough food was a problem reserved for the homeless. Yet here we were, with a home, with an income, and still not enough to put food on the table.

The realization hit me like a ton of bricks. It was shocking, embarrassing, and more than anything, deeply humbling. I felt ashamed to admit that we were struggling, but the reality was staring at me in the face. How had it come to this? What were we going to do now? Twenty-four hours without food would be a hardship for anyone, but what about for a child? For my child? That was something I could not even fathom. Letting my child go hungry was not an option I had ever considered, but here we were, teetering on that very brink.

I needed help, but the thought of asking for it was a bitter pill to swallow. It was hard to admit that we could not do it on our own. Harder still to confront the fact that we were on the edge of a crisis we had not seen coming. Pride kept me silent, but our reality was demanding action. The question was, would I let pride win, or would I do what needed to be done to take care of my family? The clock was ticking, and I had to make a choice.

At the point of desperation, I felt utterly depleted. It was as if the weight of everything was crashing down all at once, and I could barely keep my head above water. I stood in the stillness of my home, closed my eyes, and let out a deep, exasperated plea. "God, what am I going to do?" I was not sure if I truly expected an answer, or if I was just venting my frustrations, desperate for some semblance of relief. At that moment, I simply needed something, anything, to go right. Even just a flicker of hope would have been enough to keep me from sinking further into despair.

With no time to dwell on the unknown, I moved through the motions of the morning. I dressed my daughter for school, grateful beyond measure for the fact that she would at least have breakfast and lunch that day, meals that I knew she would enjoy without worry. It gave me a small comfort, knowing that she would be taken care of for a few hours. Meanwhile, I made my way to work with a mind full of questions and anxieties, trying to conjure up a solution out of thin air. I had hoped for some miraculous way to pull together dinner that evening with nothing left to spare.

As the hours wore on, I tried to stay focused, but my mind kept wandering to the empty cupboards at home. And then, as if my silent cries for help had been heard, an unexpected opportunity presented itself. During my shift, a coworker and a friend I had grown close to over the year approached me with an invitation. She was hosting a bible study at her home that evening and was planning to serve dinner for everyone attending. What caught my attention most was the fact that she had three children of her own and yet, she extended the invitation to myself, another coworker, and our families. All she asked was that we confirm the headcount before her shift ended so she could prepare accordingly.

I was stunned. It was exactly what I needed, and it could not have come at a better time. It felt like a gift dropped directly into my lap, just as I was on the brink of breaking. I could hardly believe the timing, but there it was, an open door when I needed it most.

That evening, as we arrived at my coworker's home, everything was exactly as she had promised. We gathered for a heartfelt bible study, which was followed by the most welcoming and comforting meal. I could not tell if it was the sheer relief of having something to eat or if it was the undeniable deliciousness of the food itself, but that meal tasted like a feast fit for kings. I looked across the table at my daughter, happily eating and smiling, and I felt a wave of gratitude wash over me. I quietly thanked God for this moment and thanked my coworker for her generosity. Unbeknownst to her that invitation had been the answer to my prayer.

That night marked a turning point for me. It was not just the fact that we had been fed or that the immediate crisis had been averted. It was the realization that people around us are often carrying burdens we know nothing about. I had struggled in silence, put on a brave face, and no one had any idea how close I was to the edge. Just as no one had noticed my situation, I began to understand that many of the people I encountered each day could be facing their own silent battles, hidden behind smiles and pleasantries.

I became more mindful of the fact that the struggles we face behind closed doors do not always manifest outwardly. We wear masks, blend in with the crowd, and carry on as if everything is fine even when it is not. My coworker's simple act of kindness reminded me that we never truly know what someone else is going through. Her invitation, though small in her eyes, had been life-changing for me.

Now, I carry that lesson with me wherever I go. I remind myself that even the smallest gesture can be someone's lifeline. You never know if you will be the person who offers someone their next, or their last, meal. We all have the power to be that moment of grace for another, and in doing so, we make the world a little brighter, a little kinder, and a lot more compassionate.

Self Reflection

What emotions, thoughts, or fears do you carry privately that others rarely see?

How have you experienced hopelessness, and in what ways did it shape your daily choices or outlook?

Have there been moments when hope unexpectedly returned or circumstances shifted in surprising ways?

What lessons might your unseen struggles carry that you could only understand later, after a miraculous turn or breakthrough?

How might your story of despair, if shared carefully, inspire compassion, connection, or hope in others?

Growth & Reflection

What practices help you remain open to possibilities even when you feel overwhelmed by hopelessness?

In what ways can you cultivate gratitude for the small miracles during dark periods?

If you imagined hope or a miracle as a quiet presence shrouded in your faith beside you, how would that shift your experience of despair in the future?

THE OLD SIN

Turning on the morning news is as routine as breakfast for me. It's the morning background in my grandma's house, my mom's, and mine. I find comfort in hearing weather and traffic alerts that help me prepare for the day. As I went about my morning routine, I listened selectively, waiting for relevant information to catch my ear. Sometimes, something piques my interest. Other times, the reporting feels so random that I question why I still tune in every morning. But on that particular morning, something grabbed my attention and stopped me in my tracks.

"Rudolph Bryson," the anchor announced. I froze, my ears straining in disbelief. That name. I knew it immediately, instinctively. Rudolph was one of those names you do not forget, partly because it is rare and partly because it belonged to a friend I had teased countless times. In the neighborhood most people knew him as Bam.

He opted for that nickname years ago to dodge the teasing. But I was one of the few he trusted not to tease him about his real name. So, hearing "Rudolph Bryson" on the news was not just strange, it was unsettling.

I strained to listen, hoping I had misheard. But the anchor's grim report left no doubt. Rudolph had been shot, and worse, a mutual friend of ours had been killed in the same attack. My mind reeled, struggling to comprehend. Rudolph was always the life of the party, kind-hearted and easygoing. Who would want to hurt him? Why would anyone even think of shooting him? Suddenly, all my daily preparations seemed inconsequential compared to the information I learned. Only one thing mattered now, finding out if my friend was alright.

I dialed his number, then his home, then his brother's, desperate for an answer. Each call went unanswered, and I left a trail of voicemails, trying to keep the panic out of my voice. I called a few mutual friends, but none had heard anything. It hit me that I might be the first in our circle to know. As much as I wanted to share the burden, I could not, not without knowing more. So, I waited, pacing, clutching my phone, hoping for a call to shed light on what had happened. I waited for a call back, but it never came.

A few days later, a knock rattled my front door. I peered through the peephole to see a tall figure cloaked in a dark hoodie, face partially obscured. It was him. My heart pounded as I threw open the door, relief flooding through me. "Rudolph," I breathed, ushering him inside. But the moment he stepped in, I felt a chill. His expression was not one I was used to seeing on his usually cheery face. Though I was shocked and happy to see him, a part of me regretted seeing him like this. Everything about his demeanor told me that this was real and that my friend was far from being okay.

Once he was inside my apartment, I was the first to speak. I was desperate to hear firsthand what happened. "I heard about what happened on the news," I said softly. He shook his head slowly, his eyes shadowed with a pain that words cannot capture. "You don't know the half of it," he murmured. What he told me next unraveled me. My stomach twisted as I listened, too stunned to speak, to his firsthand account of the horror he survived.

It had started as an ordinary afternoon, just a few guys hanging out, joking around. They had spent hours playing basketball, catching up, and planning for the weekend, their guard completely down. As they parted ways, Rudolph's friend Ray invited him for a quick bite. That was classic Rudolph, never one to pass on food, so he jumped in the car without a second thought.

They stopped at a small restaurant, chatting about the week ahead. On the way out, they spotted Sam, another friend, walking down the street. Sam asked for a lift, saying he only lived a block away. They all piled into Ray's car, joking, and playing music along the way as usual. Nothing felt off, not even a hint of what was to come.

As they turned onto Rudolph's street, the mood stayed light. Ray parked, singing along to the radio while Rudolph unbuckled his seatbelt and turned to say goodbye. That's when he saw it. The cold flash in Sam's eyes, his chilling resolve as he raised a gun, pointing it directly at the back of Ray's head. The bullet struck Ray, silencing his voice mid- chorus. Rudolph's outstretched hand, still in a wave goodbye, caught the second shot, and pain radiated through him, though he barely registered it as he dove down, seeking cover. Sam slipped out of the back seat and disappeared into the shadows. Rudolph laid there in silence, barely remembering to breathe, blood dripping from his hand, mind paralyzed with horror as he looked at Ray, his closest friend, lifeless beside him.

The police arrived not long after, their sirens piercing the tense silence that hung heavily in the air. But Rudolph was in no state to respond. He stood there, numb and hollow, his mind a storm of disbelief and betrayal. He had seen everything unfold, every horrific second. The attacker was not some faceless criminal or distant enemy. No, it was Sam, his friend, or at least, the man he had once called a friend, who had turned on them with a shocking, merciless violence that left Rudolph shattered. As the officers questioned him, he struggled to speak, his voice barely a whisper, his mind wrestling with an unfathomable truth.

When the news broke, announcing Rudolph's name and confirming that he was alive, he felt a new wave of fear. He knew Sam had escaped and could not shake the feeling that Sam thought he was dead as well. Sam thought he had left no witnesses. Now, knowing Rudolph had survived might have placed a target on his back. Rudolph's fear spread to his family, who now worried about his safety with a dread that shadowed their every thought and action.

I felt an immense responsibility, yet I was entirely out of my depth. How could I help someone unravel the threads of betrayal and trauma so deep they threatened to consume him? This was not ordinary heartbreak, no minor betrayal. This was literal life and deathly betrayal from someone Rudolph had trusted. There were layers of deception and cruelty that he had not even begun to

process. And while I was not a professional, trained to counsel or heal, I knew one thing. I could be a friend, a true friend, in the only way I knew how. So, I sat with him,
listening to every word he shared, no matter how long he needed to talk, no matter how dark his story became.

As he spoke, I felt the weight of his words pressing down on us both, the raw disbelief that something like this could happen. One moment he was surrounded by friends living in the moment. Seconds later he sat beside his friend. A decision and a bullet removed his friend from this life. It defied reason, challenged everything he believed about loyalty, trust, and friendship. This was not just a betrayal. It was the ultimate betrayal. One man's life was lost, another had barely escaped and in between was a shattered trust in people that might never mend.

As I sat with Rudolph, the weight of that truth settled over us. I could not fix what Sam had done, could not erase the scars, or undo the betrayal. But by being there, by listening, by sharing his burden, I hoped to remind him that not everyone in his life was untrustworthy. It was a strange quandary. I felt utterly helpless, unable to do anything to alleviate my friend's pain. He sat there, wading through a pool of helpless agony, trying to make sense of what happened.

In the following weeks, Rudolph learned he had been collateral damage in a hit not intended for him. Jealousy had ignited the murderous betrayal by his friend. Rudolph happened to be witness to the plan's execution. In the end, none of it mattered. Learning the truth made it all seem even more pointless.

Betrayal has a way of cutting deeper than any physical wound. It is a blade that pierces straight to the heart. The irony is that it can only be wielded by those closest to us, those we have allowed into our lives, into our confidence. Family members, friends, lovers, mentors, they are the ones capable of wielding that knife. They are the ones we have trusted enough to let near. And when they turn on us, the wound they leave is more than skin deep. It reaches the core of who we are, leaving a pain that, if not properly tended to, can fester and spread like an infection. Bitterness, anger, and despair can creep inside that wound, poisoning everything they touch, making healing seem impossible.

True healing from such betrayal, I have come to realize, cannot come from willpower or good intentions alone. Many try to patch the wound themselves, to hide the brokenness behind a brave face, to build walls so high that no one can ever hurt them again. But those walls only trap the pain within, preventing true recovery. Only God has the power to reach into that brokenness, to draw out the poison of bitterness, anger, and despair, and to restore a heart shattered by betrayal. Betrayal, like a dagger thrust into the back that finds its way to the heart, leaves a wound so deep that no human strength can truly repair it. Fortunately, God is not like us. He alone can lift the pain and bring genuine peace where there was only ruin. I prayed Rudolph would find the strength from God. I still believe that through God's grace, hope and healing are always possible, even in the darkest of places.

Self Reflection

What happened to cause you to feel betrayed by someone close to you, and how did it break the trust you placed in this person?

Were there subtle signs you may have overlooked, and how do you make peace with that awareness without self-blame?

Have I allowed myself to fully feel the hurt, or have I tried to suppress or rationalize it?

What boundaries did you ignore or did not have in place?

In what ways might forgiveness, not necessarily reconciliation, serve your own healing and growth?

Growth & Reflection

What lessons about trust, discernment, or human nature can you carry forward from the situation?

How do you establish healthy boundaries in the future to protect yourself from further harm?

How can your experience deepen your capacity for empathy, wisdom, or emotional resilience and how might you use those enhancements in the future.

What support systems, practices, or routines can help you release lingering pain and move forward with clarity without resentment?

THE SHIFT OF LIFE

The day began like any other, a quiet, uneventful stretch that seemed to drag on endlessly. Just another boring day, I thought to myself. There was nothing remarkable about it. To be fair, it was the tail end of summer, and most people were already busy shifting gears, preparing for the upcoming school year or settling into their fall routines. I could not blame them, really. Even I was mentally ticking off my own checklist. But at that moment, it was just a regular day, unremarkable in every sense, until a familiar sound sliced through the monotony, flipping the script entirely.

The doorbell rang. Not just any ring, though, our mailman's ring. You see, he had a signature move. Two quick, consecutive rings that always meant one thing. It was like he had his own secret code, a little unspoken language between him and the homes he delivered to. And the message today was clear as day. You might want to grab this mail, fast. I knew what that meant. Whenever he saw a payment check looking image in the envelope's address window, our mail carrier would use that special ring.

Curiosity piqued, I wandered out of my room, hoping to catch a glimpse of what was going on. But clearly, I was not fast enough. My mother had the reflexes of someone twice as invested in the mail as I was. She had already brushed past me in a blur, making a beeline for the mailbox attached to the right of our front door. She was always quick when it came to moments like these. Either she was expecting the check, or she could sense the day was about to take a sudden turn.

She yanked open the mailbox, grabbed the envelope, and within seconds, was back inside, waving it like a winning lottery ticket. "Get dressed!" she shouted, her voice echoing through the house. "We are going to the bank! Hurry up, we have errands to run!"

That was all I needed to hear. The day, once flat and uneventful, had taken a sharp turn. Suddenly, we had somewhere to be, something to do, and just like that, the boring day was history. My younger brother and I scrambled to get ready, the anticipation building. We all hurriedly got dressed and hopped in my mother's car. What had started off as just another lazy, end-of-summer day was now on the verge of becoming something entirely different.

The mood felt like a spark, a lighthearted energy that filled the car as soon as we piled in. My mom was in one of her best moods, the kind that lifts everyone else up along with it. And even the car seemed to know what kind of day it would be. Just as she turned the key, the first beats of Johnny Kemp's "Just Got Paid" burst through the speakers, almost like it had been waiting just for us. Without missing a beat, Mom cranked the volume and started singing, her shoulders swaying, fingers tapping on the steering wheel, fully immersed in the song.

My brother and I exchanged a look, and we jumped right in, singing and dancing along with her. The car became her stage, and we were the backup singers. We cruised down the street as the music spilled out of the windows as if the whole neighborhood should be in on the fun. For those few minutes, everything felt light, effortless, like all the day's worries had decided to take the day off.

We finally pulled up to the bank, still buzzing with laughter and lingering beats. My brother and I trailed behind Mom, stepping inside the cool, quiet bank lobby.

The check cashing process was a boring process of verification, signature, and endless minutes watching the seconds tick by. But today, none of it bothered us. We were still coasting on that happy high. Eventually, Mom walked away from the counter with a smile, some of the cash in hand, and the same infectious energy that had started our day.

With the bank checked off our list, we were ready for the rest of our errands. The new school year was just around the corner, and there were still plenty of last-minute essentials to grab. As we wandered through department store aisles, Mom kept ticking items off her list with the precision of someone who was on a mission. She did not pick up much for herself, though it was expected. Mom rarely bought things beyond what was necessary. She always seemed to put us first, letting her own wants take a backseat. She seemed to not mind, at least not today. Her joy was right there in her smile, in the way she hummed to herself as she searched the shelves.

After hours of wandering in and out of stores, trying on clothes, and checking off last-minute school essentials, we were wiped out and starving. Mom took one look at us, eyelids drooping, stomachs grumbling, and decided to call it a day. And as a special treat, she suggested we swing by our favorite burger spot on the way home. My brother and I perked up immediately. Eating out was rare for us, and the promise of salty fries and chocolate milkshakes was almost as exciting as the day itself had been.

As we waited for our food, relaxing in the booth and savoring the warm, delicious aroma, my brother's face suddenly shifted. Out of nowhere, he sat up straight and, with a look of absolute horror, blurted out, "I think I left the stove on at home!" My mom and I froze, trying to make sense of his words. He quickly explained how he had been cooking hot dogs right before the mail carrier showed up. In his rush to get dressed, he was not sure if he had remembered to turn the stove off before we left.

One part of my brain processed his words while the other part began doing math. How long had we been out? Four hours. Four whole hours with the stove potentially left on. My mom took a deep breath, trying to stay calm as she said, "Well, we're already headed home, so whatever's happened has likely already happened." The excitement and laughter from earlier evaporated, replaced by a thick anxiety that hung in the air. In my mind, I pictured us returning to a smoldering, blackened skeleton of our house, flames licking up the walls, the smell of smoke filling the neighborhood.

On the drive home, my imagination ran wild. I pictured everything from a tiny, manageable scorch mark on the kitchen wall to a raging fire that had already taken over the house. But there was a glimmer of hope. Maybe, just maybe, the hot dogs were still sitting in a pot of undisturbed, cold water, no harm done. I clung to that small, fragile thought as we turned onto our street, everyone in the car on high alert, eyes scanning the skyline for any trace of smoke.

As we neared the house, I felt a surge of relief. No smoke, no flames, everything looked exactly as we had left it. In fact, my brother's friends from across the street were even waiting on the front porch. Perhaps this would turn out to be like it was any other day. But just as we stepped out of the car, our relief was ripped away. His friends jumped up, shouting, "Hurry! We can hear your smoke alarm going off! Mom fumbled with her keyring, hands shaking as she tried to find the right key. The seconds felt like hours with the chirping of the smoke detector blaring from inside the house. Finally, she found the key and unlocked the door. But as she pushed it open, a thick, dark cloud of smoke rolled out towards me, filling the doorway in a choking plume.

Instinct took over, and before I knew what my body was doing, I turned and was running across the street as fast as I could, straight to a neighbor's house. I burst through the door, barely pausing to breathe as I shouted, "Our house is on fire! Call the fire department!" The neighbor did not hesitate, grabbing her phone and dialing, though she looked at me with a mix of concern and curiosity. She asked what happened, but I could not linger. There was no time. I dashed back to the house, where my mom, brother, and his friends were gathered near the doorway, all peering into the smoky entry.

Just as I arrived, we heard the sound of sirens cutting through the air. Within moments, the fire trucks were there, and finally, I could let go of the breath I had been holding. Thankfully the fire station was a few minutes down the street from our home. Neighbors started to gather around, asking questions, but we did not have many answers to give. We just kept it simple. "The house filled up with smoke while we were out." My thoughts were flooded with the idea of us losing every earthly possession we had. Starting over from nothing was a hardship I desperately wanted to be spared from.

Eventually, a firefighter came over to give us an update. There was smoke damage primarily in the kitchen.

Thankfully, no structural harm. The stove, however, was a different story. As we listened, firefighters emerged from the house carrying what was left of our stove. It had become a concave, crumpled heap of metal. They set it on the side porch, still smoldering. The firemen were baffled at the quality and craftsmanship of the stove. Miraculously it withstood the heat for hours without combusting into flames. Whether it was a true miracle or not I was grateful. Of all the worst scenarios I had imagined, this one had not even crossed my mind. It was the best possible fire related outcome.

    As I stood outside, our home still swirling with the aftereffects of smoke, firemen bustling through our front yard, and neighbors filling the sidewalks, an odd clarity settled over me. I felt the pull of something I needed to do. Quietly, I crossed the street, back to the neighbor's house where, not so long ago, I had run to in desperation. I was grateful the neighbor had listened without hesitation and called for help, no questions asked. Now, with the crisis controlled, I took the time to thank her, to answer her questions, to let her curiosity settle. It was a small gesture, but one I hoped conveyed my gratitude for her presence when I had needed it most.

Finally, as the last fire truck pulled away and neighbors drifted back to their homes, I returned to ours, taking in the stillness of what remained. The smell of smoke lingered in the air, heavy, undeniable, a physical reminder of what could have been. And so, I found myself reflecting on the day, and the strange, sudden turns it had taken, like an unpredictable string of moments veering off course with every unexpected turn.

It struck me then how easily life can shift, how our days can be irrevocably altered by a single, seemingly insignificant decision or chance occurrence. One forgotten stove burner, one moment of inattention, and suddenly the future we assumed was ours to control had splintered off in another direction entirely. We tend to imagine that life is stable, that the hours unfold predictably, but that illusion only holds until one tiny variable changes it all. In that shift, an action as simple as stepping out the door or as careless as leaving the stove on, everything we rely on can turn upside down.

Isn't it humbling, then, to think of how much our lives depend on these unseen, often unacknowledged threads that hold our world together? We can plan, prepare, and hold expectations as tightly as we want, but every single moment carries the potential to unravel them.

This realization is not one of hopelessness, though. Instead, it speaks to life's raw, unfiltered beauty. It's a beauty that forces us to accept change, to find growth in uncertainty, and perhaps even to appreciate that our journey is defined by its twists as much as by its destinations.

In that moment, I understood that we are all separated by variables, by decisions we did and did not make, by events that happened, and by lives we could have lived but did not. Yet somehow, we keep moving, trusting the ground beneath us, only to learn that every step can shift. It is an exercise in resilience, a lesson in humility. And if we can accept this, perhaps we find freedom in knowing that life does not require perfection or certainty, but only a willingness to walk forward, even when we do not know the way.

Self Reflection

What event or moment in your life felt completely unexpected, and how did it change your trajectory?

What assumptions or plans were disrupted by this unexpected change?

Did this shift highlight strengths or resilience you didn't know you had?

What lessons, insights, or opportunities emerged from this unexpected event?

In what ways has the change revealed what truly matters versus what you once thought did?

Growth & Reflection

How has surviving or adapting to this sudden change strengthened your character?

If you could speak to yourself before the shift occurred, what guidance or reassurance would you offer?

How can you honor both the disruption of the event and the growth it brought into your life?

THE TALK

Birds of the same feather is what we were. I used to think our similar sense of humor drew us together, but it was deeper than that. Our personalities seemed bridged by an unspoken familiarity between us. Between Christina and I, she was the more outspoken one. I often teased that instead of a filter, God gave her a faucet because once she had a thought, it flowed from her lips like water from a faucet.

Christina and I worked together, which made work so much more enjoyable. It felt less like a job and more like an ongoing conversation threaded with laughter. The hours went by like minutes and the work week felt like a few days. We talked about everything and laughed at anything. Coworkers, the job itself, our families, histories, television shows, and our day-to-day issues were all up for discussion. Depending on the day, we may have touched on every subject. Neither of us had to think twice or offer a disclaimer on a topic that may have been a sensitive issue for some people. After one year of working like that, it felt as if we had known one another for years.

One day, Christina received a phone call. Usually, her telephone voice and demeanor were giveaways to whom she was taking to. This time I could not tell. The way she answered and responded signaled to me that it was not business or a personal phone call. "Yes, this is she" followed by a "yes, I can talk now" was a clear sign that it was not work related. It was sometimes inconvenient to work in a small space. I focused on my work duties to tune out Christina in the background. If it were a personal call, she deserved as much privacy as I could give her in that moment. I turned to another coworker and struck up a conversation. We could both use the distraction from Christina's voice echoing against the silence. Besides, if she wanted me to know what was going on, she would tell me so.

Christina ended her phone call and returned to her work duties. Our desks were close enough so that I could see the distracted concern on her face. I wanted to show concern but not come across as prying. I decided to extend an olive branch of "Chrissy, are you good"? It was the right mix of friendly, mixed with concern, and a touch of simple and sweet. Christina responded with "yeah I'm fine". We left it at that and continued chatting and working through our day.

The next day, things were a little different. To start off, Christina was not at work. Our manager asked the other members of our team to offset Christina's workload while she was out of the office. The added workload was no problem, but I felt there may be a problem elsewhere. I quickly texted Christina to check in with her. Perhaps she, or one of her kids were sick. I just wanted to make sure she was okay and, on the mend, if that was the case. It took a few minutes for her response. When the text came in, I wasn't sure of what to make of it. It simply read, "I'm not sick I just needed to figure some things out. I'll be back to work in a day or two."

After a quick mental recollection of my and Christina's conversations I reflected on what issues were going on in her life. I could not recall anything in my memory that would have called for Christina to miss work. Regardless of what was going on I was more concerned with the well-being of my friend. I sent a brief reply to her message "I'm here for you if you need me just say the word and I'll be there."

After three more days of work without Christina, I was happy to see her seated at her desk on Friday. With a smile beaming across my face, I greeted her with "Welcome back I missed you." "Missed you too girl" she responded in a cutesy whisper. We worked through the morning in sync with our usual routine. By lunchtime we both decided to go to a neighboring conference room and eat in instead of going out. There was something calming about retreating to a conference room for an hour of lunch time. It ensured us privacy, quiet and seclusion from all reminders of work.

Inside the conference room, the light mood I expected took on a different feeling. Christina turned to me and said I need to tell you something. Her voice was serious, and her face doubled down on the weight of the subject Christina prepared to speak on. She began by telling me the phone call she received at work the other day was from her daughter's school. The teacher requested a conference that evening after school.

When Christina arrived at the conference, the teacher did her best to prepare her for a difficult conversation. Christina's daughter had begun to struggle in class. The teacher noticed a change in her and began to nurture her daughter with more encouragement and patience. Her daughter seemed to respond well to the support. After some time, Christina's daughter felt comfortable enough to open up to the teacher. She asked her teacher to do something for her that she did not know how to do herself. She asked her teacher to tell her mother something she could not. Her stepfather had been assaulting her for years and she wanted it to stop.

Christina's voice trembled as she asked me how it was possible for her to not know or notice? My mouth opened to speak but nothing came out. I was too stunned. When the tears began to flow from Christinas eyes, I snapped out of it and began to support my friend. She told me that her husband of seven years, the father of her son, began assaulting her daughter when she was younger, and it continued to escalate over the years. His assaults were increasing, and she feared for the safety of her younger sister.

Christina had no reason to doubt her daughter's account. The details the child shared with her teacher were far too vivid and specific to be fabricated. She thanked the teacher for bringing the truth to light and admitted, with a heavy heart, that she felt like the worst mother alive for not protecting her daughter from such harm. Overwhelmed with guilt, she asked herself a barrage of questions. What signs were there that I failed to see? How could I not recognize the true nature of the man I chose to marry?

Despite all her initial efforts to ensure he was a good man and a suitable stepfather, her judgment had failed her.

Christina realized that her self-blame, while human, would not help her daughter. The best protection she could offer now lay not in rewriting the past but in ensuring her daughter was and felt protected. Christina filed a police report and confronted her husband. His response was to blame the daughter and when that did not work, he ran away. Literally, mid conversation or argument, he bolted for the door and ran away.

Desperate for answers, Christina reached out to his family. What she uncovered was an even deeper betrayal. His relatives, his own blood, had known about past allegations involving children. Whispers of abuse had followed him for years, yet no one had warned her. They had kept their children away from him, but they had never told her why. Their excuse? "It wasn't our place." Christina unleashed her fury. They may not have committed the crime, but their silence had enabled it. Their unwillingness to speak had left her daughter vulnerable to a monster she had unknowingly invited into her home.

In the days that followed, Christina did everything she could to protect her children. She changed the locks. Installed cameras. Created a support system with counselors and family. She sat down with her daughter and made her a promise. No more secrets. No more silence. That man was never coming near her again. As she told me all of this, I saw something shift in her. The guilt and pain were still there, but beneath them, something stronger had taken root. Determination. She could not change the past, but she would do everything in her power to ensure her daughter's future was safe.

We talked for hours, dissecting every moment, every missed sign. Christina had once thought her husband was a good man. Now, in hindsight, she could see manipulation in the way he had positioned himself as a caring stepfather. Under the light of the truth, it was easy to see how he had built trust before shattering it. What once looked like kindness was, under the harsh light of truth, a predator's strategy cloaked in innocence

Christina and her daughter's story is devastatingly familiar. I have seen it in the faces of too many others. Mothers, fathers, children scarred by the same evil. It is a darkness that thrives in silence, in secrecy, in the spaces where trust is given too freely. And that is why we must speak out against it.

If you are a parent, never assume that danger could never touch your child. Evil does not come with a warning label. It wears the faces of those we trust most. Listen to your children. Believe them. Teach them that their voice matters, that no one, no matter how kind or beloved, has the right to make them feel unsafe.

Predators rely on silence. They count on doubt, on hesitation, on the fear of being wrong. But I would rather be wrong a thousand times than miss the one moment that could have saved a child. Christina did not allow silence to win. She chose to fight, to protect, to believe in her daughter even when the truth shattered her world. That is the kind of courage we all need. It's the courage to ask hard questions, to listen, and to act. Because the cost of silence is far too high.

A little discomfort or hurt feelings are a small price to pay for the safety and well-being of your child. Be bold, be unapologetic, and choose their protection over politeness. The vigilance you show today could be the shield that spares your child from unthinkable harm tomorrow.

Self Reflection

How will you discern the difference between healthy caution and unnecessary fear when it comes to your child's safety?

What environments, relationships, or situations raise red flags for you, and how do you respond to those instincts?

In what ways can you teach your child to recognize and trust their own boundaries?

How can you model self-respect and healthy boundaries, so your child learns by example?

In what ways can you give your child language and tools to speak up if they ever feel unsafe or uncomfortable?

Growth & Reflection

What fears, if any, do you carry from your own past experiences, and how do they influence your protective instincts?

How can you create a home environment where your child knows they can always share anything without fear of judgment or punishment?

How do you want your child to remember your guidance and protection as they grow into independence?

THE UNEXPLAINABLE

I should have known from the start that the day would unfold in the strangest way possible. It began with an oddness I could not quite place. There was a peculiar shift in the usual rhythm of things. For reasons unknown to me, my mother had allowed a friend from our old neighborhood to come by for a visit. Alicia was among the list of the reasons my mother had packed us up and moved the family across town. Alicia was a rebellious friend I met in elementary school who seemed to have a knack for being in situations my mother did not want me in. Yet here she was back in our lives for the day.

As if that were not strange enough, we had a car that day. This was unusual for us. My family was typically in between cars, trading one burned out junker in for the next. Having a working vehicle at our disposal was not common. Since we had a guest visiting, my mother opted to take my brothers, Alicia, and me out for the day. And just like that, we piled into the car one by one. My youngest brother claimed the front seat. He had to be within arm's reach of my mother so she could keep an eye on him. Alicia, my older brother, and I crammed into the backseat of that old car. It was a beat-up vehicle that my older cousins loved to mock because of its oversized length and width. I did not mind at all since it kept us off the city bus and managed to get us where we needed to go.

With the engine rumbling beneath us, we set off, my mother steering us through the streets she knew so well. She had grown up in the city and knew all the back roads, shortcuts, and secret routes to avoid the thickening traffic. The radio blared, and she sang along, carefree, and confident as always. We were on one of those backstreets, just a few miles from downtown, when the day took a dramatic, unsettling turn.

Suddenly, my mother slammed on the brakes, bringing the car to an abrupt halt. Ahead of us, a woman in the middle of the street was waving her arms frantically, signaling for my mother to stop. Bold and fearless as she was, my mother was also quite street smart. I expected her to keep driving. Then again, she was also the type to stop for someone in need, especially a fellow woman in need. I leaned forward, peering around her to get a better look at the woman outside. She was unlike anyone I had ever seen, at least not in real life. She was dressed in a lavish fur coat, not one of those faux furs you might see, but the real deal. I promise it looked like an authentic chinchilla coat, something you would only ever see in the movies. To top it off, she wore oversized tinted glasses and layers of gold jewelry that sparkled even in the dull afternoon light. All I could think was, "Why is this movie star walking around in this part of town?"

But she was not a movie star plastered on a screen. She was a real person with a real problem, in need of real help. Her words rushed out in a panicked jumble: "Gunshots... my husband... shot... help, please!" It was not a glamorous scene unfolding before us. It was something far darker and more real. She pleaded with my mother for help, explaining that her husband was an undercover police officer who had been shot multiple times. They needed to get out of there fast. And then, my mother did something I would have bet all my adolescent possessions against her doing. She paused for a moment, and then she told the woman, "Come on, get in quick."

The woman shouted toward the back of a building, and a man appeared, half-running, half-staggering toward us. His injuries were in multiple areas of his body. If you had asked me that morning, I would have sworn my mother would never let strangers into the car, let alone under such terrifying circumstances with us in the car. But there we were, in the middle of a bizarre day, making room in the backseat for two strangers, one whose body was riddled with fresh gunshot wounds.

In the backseat, Alicia, my brother, and I shifted over to make room. I was by the window, farthest from the bleeding man and his wife. Alicia and my brother were not so lucky. The couple pressed in close to them as they squeezed into the car. I felt a strange sense of relief that they got in using the door opposite me. It was not my proudest moment, but I was particularly squeamish around bleeding people. Once inside, my mother sped away and asked which hospital they wanted to go to. They declined the hospital and asked to be driven downtown to the police station.

As we drove away, the woman began spilling out her story in a frantic rush. She and her husband had been on a date when he noticed something suspicious, a robbery in progress. He intervened, and a gunfight erupted. Her husband, the undercover police officer, was outnumbered and tried to retreat with his wife from the scene. Right before we arrived, her husband ran out of bullets and sent his wife running to safety. Desperate and trying to figure out a way to safety, she saw our car and decided to flag us down.

Her husband had been shot in both legs, arm, and even through his ear. As she called out the wounds, I could not help looking at each body part to verify the story. I saw the blood dripping from his wounds, staining his clothes and the seat beneath him. His left earlobe was mangled and bloody. His black leather jacket had a couple of small bullet holes in it. The woman, however, was unharmed. Her luxurious fur coat remained pristine, not a single drop of blood on it.

Within minutes, we arrived at the police station, where the couple hurried out of the car, thanking my mother profusely. Their departure exposed the bloodstains left behind in the backseat. Alicia and my brother scrunched closer to me, trying to avoid the mess. Again, I was so thankful for my window seat on the opposite end of the car that day. Though the entire event had taken less than fifteen minutes, it felt like an hour-long, cinematic sequence. I was both terrified and enthralled, hardly able to believe what had just happened.

After dropping them off, we could not contain our excitement. Everyone began to talk at once about how crazy that experience was. By the time we got home, we were all talked out. We all went our separate ways, quietly processing what had just happened. I tried to talk to Alicia about it, but she was upset, shaken by the experience of sitting next to the bleeding man. My older brother was irritated with the situation, convinced we could have been shot at ourselves. But my mother simply said she was glad she had been there at the right moment to help.

Over the next few days, we scoured the newspapers and watched the news, expecting to see some mention of the incident. Maybe there would be a story about the shootout, an update on the couple's condition. But there was nothing. It was as though the event had vanished, leaving no trace behind. We had witnessed it all, yet there was no official record of it. Perhaps he was still undercover or there was an ongoing investigation. Whatever the fallout was, I could not make sense of it.

Years passed, as the memory of that day lingered in the back of my mind. One day, I brought it up with my mother, expecting her to remember it vividly. But to my shock, she had no recollection of it whatsoever. I detailed every moment, every strange turn of events, but still, nothing. She denied it, saying she would never pick up hitchhikers, especially with us kids in the car. Determined to prove I was not imagining it she called my brother to ask if he remembered. He excitedly confirmed my story, recounting the details just as I had. My mother was stunned, bewildered that such a vivid memory could have slipped from her mind entirely.

Even now, after all these years, I find myself grappling with a question that refuses to fade. Why does my mother have no memory of that day? I can still see it vividly, the man, riddled with gunshot wounds, defenseless and out of ammo, being hunted down on a desolate backstreet. The odds of survival at that moment were impossibly slim. And yet, we were there. We stopped to help, and I am convinced that without us, he would not have made it. That couple's fate seemed to hinge on the sheer timing and improbability of our car taking a short cut on a desolate street that rarely sees traffic. My mother's split-second decision to stop the car and even more, to let them in was beyond us all. They were fortunate. No, it was more than fortunate. We were meant to be there. Of that, I am certain.

Life often hands us moments that resist logic with experiences that feel orchestrated yet leave us questioning the script. Why were they saved when so many others in the world endure similar perils without rescue? Was there some unseen significance to their lives, something greater that we were unwittingly part of? These questions linger in the back of my mind, unresolved but ever present.

Perhaps it is human nature to search for meaning, to wrestle with the interplay of fate, chance, and choice. Some might chalk it up to coincidence, a random twist of events. But I cannot believe it is as simple as that. Moments like these further prove to me that there is a God, a divine presence that is very real and undeniably powerful. The peculiarities of that day, the oddities that defied logic and explanation, were not random occurrences, nor were they merely the result of chance. I witnessed the events of that day as they fell into place with an almost eerie precision. As though some unseen hand had carefully orchestrated each moment, weaving them together to form a tapestry of interconnected choices and outcomes. We were in the right place at the right time, and it was not because of coincidence or blind luck. It felt as if every twist and turn of that day had been deliberately arranged, part of a larger plan that we could not fully comprehend but were nevertheless a part of.

Over time, I have learned to embrace these miraculous moments, as opportunities that strengthen my faith. While I may never fully understand why certain events unfold as they do or what greater purpose they serve.

I take solace in the belief that there is a divine presence, alive and active, weaving through our lives. This presence, who I know as God, works effectively and persistently, even when the answers evade us. It is often in these very moments of witnessing the miracles that evade our full comprehension, that our faith is sparked, reminding us that we are not walking this path alone.

Faith is always present and readily available, encouraging us to trust in the unseen, to believe that there is a guiding hand, even in the most uncertain times. And it is that faith we must turn to every day, drawing strength, seeking guidance, and finding help within it to navigate the twists and turns of life. We are not asked to understand everything, but we are invited to trust that with God, and through God, all things are made possible. This belief is like a firm hand outstretched to guide us against the constant twists and turns of life, offering hope, peace, and purpose along our journey.

Self Reflection

When have you experienced being in the right place at the right time in a way you couldn't have orchestrated yourself?

How did those moments make you feel about God's presence and care in your life?

Were there "small details" that later revealed themselves to be part of a bigger divine plan?

How often do you pause to recognize God's hand in what others might call chance or coincidence?

In what ways have unexplainable moments strengthened your trust in God's timing?

What keeps you from seeing the divine in everyday life, and how can you become more attentive to it?

Growth & Reflection

What does it mean for you to walk in expectancy, believing God may be working in ways you cannot yet see?

Which unexplainable experiences still fill you with gratitude whenever you remember them?

How can you honor God for orchestrating these moments through prayer, testimony, or action?

What practices can you adopt to stay open, watchful, and grateful for the ways God continues to move in your life?

THE PERSPECTIVE

I hope that as you have turned these pages, you have found not only enjoyment but also a deeper sense of meaning and connection in the stories I have shared. Each story stands alone, a distinct narrative with its own characters, settings, and emotions. Yet, as different as they may seem, they are all bound together by a single, unbreakable thread. It's a thread that reflects the universal truths of the human experience. My hope is that, through these stories, you have glimpsed new perspectives, discovered insights that resonate with your own journey, and perhaps even found a quiet wisdom in the lessons each tale offers. Life, after all, is a shared journey. Though the details of our paths differ, the essence of our experiences, struggles, triumphs, and moments of growth binds us together. None of us walks this road alone.

Some of the stories highlight people at their best and their worst. You may have heard the saying, "Hurt people hurt people." It is a poignant reminder of how our own pain can ripple outward, often unintentionally wounding others. Yet the truth goes deeper. The reality is, regular people hurt people. Not just the broken or the bruised, but all of us. We navigate this chaotic, beautiful world, colliding into one another sometimes with gentleness, sometimes with harm.

These collisions are rarely premeditated and almost never fair, but they are inevitable. However, just as we have the capacity to hurt, we also hold within us the power to heal. A kind word, a shared moment, a compassionate act are the ways we repair the cracks in each other's armor. At our core, we are beings designed for connection, and it is through these connections that we find meaning, purpose, and ultimately, a sense of belonging.

Still, the reality is that people do not always meet us as their best selves. They can be careless with their words, thoughtless in their actions, or distant when we need them most. In those moments, it is easy to feel hurt, misunderstood, or even abandoned. But there is a hidden gift in these interactions, however painful they may seem. Every encounter we have, whether in joy or with sorrow, carries within it a lesson waiting to be uncovered. These lessons are not always obvious, and they rarely come without discomfort, but they are invaluable. Each person we meet is a teacher of sorts, offering us insights into ourselves and the world around us. What we do with these lessons, how we interpret them, how we allow them to shape us, is ultimately our choice.

Life is, in many ways, is an ever-evolving classroom. From the moment we take our first breath until our very last, we are students in the school of existence, continuously learning and adapting. Some lessons come gently, wrapped in moments of joy and peace, while others arrive as storms, forcing us to confront our deepest fears and vulnerabilities. Yet every experience, no matter how challenging, carries the potential for growth. The key lies in our willingness to be open, to see not just the pain or the joy but the deeper truth each moment offers. In this classroom of life, the curriculum is vast and varied, and not every lesson will resonate. That is okay. Take what serves you and leave what does not.

As we move forward on our respective paths, it is important to remember that while the roads may diverge, the purpose of the journey remains universal. We are here to love, to learn, to grow, and to find meaning in each step we take. Every triumph and failure, every fleeting moment of connection or conflict, contributes to the story we are writing with our lives. And perhaps one of the greatest lessons of all is that life, with all its imperfections, is an extraordinary gift. It invites us to evolve, to forgive, to build, and most importantly, to cherish the beauty of our shared humanity. In this, we find not just the meaning of the stories we tell but the essence of who we are.

About the Author

Erica Stephens is a passionate storyteller and advocate for the vulnerable. With a unique blend of military and civilian life experience, Erica gained a perspective that is grounded and empathetic, shaping the way she writes and the causes she champions. Her work is guided by the firm belief of empowering others through sharing knowledge and wisdom to spark change. Every piece she writes is an invitation, to reflect, to act, and to uplift those who often go unseen.

When she's not writing, Erica can be found soaking up everyday moments with her family, discovering new places, and drawing inspiration from the world around her. At her core, she is committed to leaving a meaningful legacy, one story, one lesson, and one voice at a time.

www.ingramcontent.com/pod-product-compliance
Lightning Source LLC
Chambersburg PA
CBHW060822050426
42453CB00008B/544